30

to

Understanding

the

Bhagavad Gita

~

A Complete, Simple, and Step-by-Step Guide to the Million-Year-Old Confidential Knowledge

~

HARI CHETAN

Disclaimers: This book is intended to provide accurate information concerning the subject matter covered. However, the author and the publisher accept no responsibility for inaccuracies or omissions, and the author and the publisher specifically disclaim any liability, loss, or risk, whether personal, financial, or otherwise, that is incurred as a result, directly or indirectly, from the use and/or application of the contents of this book.

Moreover, the author and the publisher of this book do not intend to hurt the sentiments of anyone, including any religion, ethnic group, caste, creed, sect, organization, company, and individual. They respect all religions and ideologies and accept no responsibility if anyone is hurt by the contents of this book.

Note: Throughout this book, the author has used the masculine gender only for ease in writing and such use is not intended to undermine the feminine gender or a third gender by any means. The principles and methods discussed in this book apply to all genders equally.

A Gift for You

In the daily commotion that characterizes our lives nowadays, it is quite easy to lose track of oneself. And so it is important for us to maintain our mental equilibrium by connecting with our spiritual selves on a regular basis.

Download Hari Chetan's **free Bhagavad Gita Workbook** designed especially for the readers of his books.

This workbook will help you test your knowledge of the core concepts given in the Bhagavad Gita, and to keep you on track in your spiritual journey.

Try it. It's free to download and is very useful!

Visit **www.harichetan.com** to download.

Thoughts of Intellectuals on the Bhagavad Gita

"When doubts haunt me, when disappointments stare me in the face, and I see not one ray of hope on the horizon, I turn to Bhagavad Gita and find a verse to comfort me; and I immediately begin to smile in the midst of overwhelming sorrow. Those who meditate on the Gita will derive fresh joy and new meanings from it every day." ~ Mahatma Gandhi

"The marvel of the Bhagavad Gita is its truly beautiful revelation of life's wisdom which enables philosophy to blossom into religion." ~ Hermann Hesse

"(The Bhagavad Gita is) one of the most clear and comprehensive summaries of perennial philosophy ever revealed; hence its enduring value is subject not only to India but to all of humanity." ~ Aldous Huxley

"That the spiritual man need not be a recluse, that union with the divine life may be achieved and maintained in the midst of worldly affairs, that the obstacles to that union lie not outside us but within us — such is the central lesson of the Bhagavad Gita." ~ Annie Besant

"In the morning I bathe my intellect in the stupendous and cosmogonal philosophy of the Bhagavad Gita in comparison with which our modern world and its literature seem puny and trivial." ~ Henry David Thoreau

"I owed a magnificent day to the Bhagavad Gita. It was as if an empire spoke to us, nothing small or unworthy, but large, serene, consistent, the voice of an old intelligence which in another age and climate had pondered and thus disposed of the same questions which exercise us." ~ Ralph Waldo Emerson

"Bhagavad Gita is a true scripture of the human race, a living creation rather than a book, with a new message for every age and a new meaning for every civilization." ~ Sri Aurobindo

"The most beautiful, perhaps the only true philosophical song existing in any known tongue ... perhaps the deepest and loftiest thing the world has to show." ~ Wilhelm von Humboldt

"I am 90% through the Bhagavad Gita ... My inner Arjuna is being channelled." ~ Will Smith

"The Bhagavad Gita deals essentially with the spiritual foundation of human existence. It is a call of action to meet the obligations and duties of life; yet keeping in view the spiritual nature and grander purpose of the universe." ~ Jawaharlal Nehru

"I hesitate not to pronounce the Gita a performance of great originality, of sublimity of conception, reasoning and diction almost unequalled; and a single exception, amongst all the known religions of mankind." ~ Lord Warren Hastings

"Those are spiritual things to reflect upon yourself, life, the world around you and see things the other way. I thought it (the Bhagavad Gita) was quite appropriate." ~ Sunita Williams

The Bhagavad Gita Series

Book 1: Bhagavad Gita - The Perfect Philosophy: 15 Reasons That Make the Song of God the Most Scientific Ideology

Book 2: Bhagavad Gita (in English): The Authentic English Translation for Accurate and Unbiased Understanding

Book 3: 30 Days to Understanding the Bhagavad Gita: A Complete, Simple, and Step-by-Step Guide to the Million-Year-Old Confidential Knowledge

Book 4: The Bhagavad Gita Summarized and Simplified: A Comprehensive and Easy-to-Read Summary of the Divine Song of God

Book 5: Mind Management through the Bhagavad Gita: Master your Mindset in 21 Days and Discover Unlimited Happiness and Success

All Books: Bhagavad Gita (In English) – The Complete Collection: 5-Books-in-1

DEDICATED TO

All Spiritual Seekers

Willing to Learn

Names of Lord Krishna mentioned in the Bhagavad Gita

Achyuta — One who is changeless

Devesha — The Lord of lords

Govinda — One who gives pleasure to the cows; Knower of the activities of the senses

Hari — The absorber of all sorrows and pains

Hrishikesha — The Lord of the senses

Janardana — One who afflicts felons; The one who grants the prayers of devotees

Keshava — The slayer of demon Keshi

Krishna — The all-attractive one

Madhava — The husband of Laxmi, the goddess of fortune

Madhusudana — The slayer of demon Madhu

Purushuttama — The best of all men; The supreme person

Varshneya — Descendant of Vrishni

Vasudeva — The Lord; Son of Vasudeva

Vishnu — The all-pervading Lord

Vishwamurte — The form of the entire universe

Yadava — Descendant of Yadu

Names of Arjuna mentioned in the Bhagavad Gita

Anagha — One who is sinless

Arjuna — One who is pure or white

Dhananjaya — Winner of wealth

Gudakesha — Conqueror of sleep

Kaunteya — Son of Kunti

Kiriti — The one who dones the glorious crown given by Indra

Mahabaho — Mighty-armed one

Pandava — Son of Pandu

Parantapa — Scorcher of enemies

Partha — Son of Pritha (Kunti)

Savyasachi — An archer capable of shooting even with the left hand

Table of Contents

Introduction

There are some questions that we humans have always sought answers to.

- Who am I?
- What is the purpose of my life?
- Is there a God?
- If yes, where does He live and what does He look like?
- Why can't we see God?
- What is death?
- Is there life after death?

... and so on.

We have been searching for the answers to these questions from the time we gained intelligence. We have sometimes turned to religion for answers and sometimes to philosophy. Sometimes we have tried to leverage our intuitions, and at other times, we have sought answers from science.

In the meantime, our lives have become much more complicated. For the last few thousand years, we have kept ourselves occupied in building empires and fighting wars without regard for rationality. And over the last century, we have focused our efforts on accelerating our lives to the point where most of us no longer have time for things like spirituality.

We have almost stopped asking these questions. Spirituality has been reduced to our morning prayers, which we say absently while stressing about our long to-do lists for the day. We are operating on autopilot. And things are only getting worse.

This, however, does not surprise me in the least; as this is precisely what the Vedas, the oldest spiritual texts, predicted. *Veda* is a Sanskrit word that means "knowledge," and the Vedas contain the most authentic knowledge in the universe. According to the Vedic scriptures, in the *Kaliyuga* (the age in which we are currently living), people will only work to acquire wealth to satisfy their material needs, and will only live to fulfill their never-ending worldly desires. The majority will ignore spirituality and religion. As a result, the environment will become unsuitable for spiritual development.

The good news is that, with God's help, a committed spiritual seeker will always find a way. Whoever sincerely seeks answers to the most important questions about human life and its purpose will definitely receive God's counsel, and He will help him gravitate toward the most credible sources of spiritual knowledge.

And the fact that you chose to read a book about the Bhagavad Gita over the millions of romance, fantasy, and thriller novels available for your entertainment shows that you are a true seeker of enlightening knowledge. Congratulations!

What is the Bhagavad Gita?

I'll give you a quick answer now, and the rest will be revealed over the next thirty days as you work your way through the chapters.

The Bhagavad Gita is the comprehensive instruction manual provided by God to us for living a perfect life in this material world.

The Bhagavad Gita (meaning "the Song of God") is the oldest and the most authoritative source of wisdom in the universe. I have given this topic its own chapter in this book. But for the time being, keep in mind that the information you are about to receive is not some made-up New Age nonsense. It is divine, original, and unadulterated. Lord Krishna imparted this knowledge for the first time millions of years ago, when He created the universe. And He repeated it five thousand years ago for the benefit of those who would live in the present era (more on this on Day 25).

The Bhagavad Gita is a collection of all the wisdom contained in the Vedas, the divine literature, that we need to have to fulfill our life's purpose. The Bhagavad Gita has seven hundred and one verses separated into eighteen chapters in which Lord Krishna explains our true identity and the sole purpose of our lives. He also reveals why He is the God, what His virtues are, and what His true form is. In short, the Bhagavad Gita provides all the knowledge that a seeker of truth may require. Understanding it leads to wisdom. Acting on it leads to freedom.

I am not going to go into detail about the magnificence of the Bhagavad Gita here, since the only way to understand it is to experience it. And this book is designed to provide you with that experience.

The purpose of this book

There are a variety of books about the Bhagavad Gita that we can read. In my own quest for spiritual wisdom, I read over a hundred books on this subject. But the biggest issue I discovered was that there was a significant lack of a step-by-step learning structure for the students of this great spiritual guide. I realized, because of the lack of a proper handbook, students became confused and found it difficult to integrate the different concepts presented in the Bhagavad Gita.

Most books about the Bhagavad Gita presented a verse-by-verse commentary. Reading the Bhagavad Gita this way can be challenging for a beginner. In my opinion, only an experienced seeker with a thorough understanding of the true spirit of the Bhagavad Gita should attempt this.

I also noticed that practically every book about the Bhagavad Gita, whether it was a verse-by-verse commentary or an explanation of its teachings, was written in a difficult-to-understand language. A book written in a simpler style that appealed to readers at all levels of consciousness was needed.

So I decided to fill these gaps myself. And the result is in your hands.

This book is designed to assist you, no matter where you are in your spiritual journey. It covers all of the information found in the Bhagavad Gita in a way that makes it easier to understand and remember. If you are a beginner, this book will undoubtedly help you in avoiding any confusion that may occur when reading the Bhagavad Gita verse by verse. I've kept the book relatively short, keeping in mind how busy most of us are in today's world. You will learn something new every day, and it will all add up to create the desired knowledge base, which will be both complete and powerful.

Getting the most out of this book

Over the next thirty days, you will be progressing through the knowledge conveyed in the Bhagavad Gita by Lord Krishna in a systematic, step-by-step manner.

Because the Bhagavad Gita challenges many of our preconceived notions, it is critical that you approach it with an open and accepting attitude. It is important and can make a significant difference in the amount of knowledge you gain from this book. If you've read my book *Bhagavad Gita – The Perfect Philosophy*, you'll know why reading the Bhagavad Gita with a welcoming mind is so crucial. As the Buddhists say, your glass is too full. Unless you empty your glass, there will be no room for anything else. While reading this book, you may need to empty your glasses many times.

(I strongly advise you to read *Bhagavad Gita - The Perfect Philosophy*. Its ebook version is available for free on my website and with most major ebook retailers. This brief book will help you build a great deal of faith in the Bhagavad Gita's teachings and put you in the right mindset to absorb them.)

You should also keep in mind that the Bhagavad Gita is *not* a religion-specific book. In other words, it is not intended for adherents of a specific religion. Religion can be blinding and deafening. The truth, on the other hand, is always pure. So, when reading this book, put religion aside.

The following is an excerpt from *Bhagavad Gita - The Perfect Philosophy* which mostly holds true for this book as well:

But why should you care to read the Bhagavad Gita and understand its philosophy if you are not a Hindu or do not believe in religion or God?

No religion or belief stops us from exploring further.

I am a Hindu by birth. But that did not stop me from reading the Bible, the Quran, the Dhammapada, and a slew of other non-Hindu scriptures.

Rather than adhering to any faith or philosophy by default, I believe in learning about different ideologies with an unbiased mind, and then adhering to the one that appeals the most to the seeker, holding utmost respect for all the other beliefs as well.

We should be open to ideas we have not heard before and accept the ones we believe have validity. The only way we can progress is by getting out of our comfort zones. That is the only way we can broaden our horizons and live more fulfilling lives.

My goal in this book is to make you aware of the philosophy that I have found to be the most enlightening one in my several years of research in the fields of spirituality and religion.

In any case, the Bhagavad Gita is not a religious book; rather, it teaches a very practical and logical way of living. Its philosophy and teachings can be followed by adherents of any ideology. The Bhagavad Gita (meaning "the Song of God") contains the teachings given by Lord Krishna to Prince Arjuna on the battlefield of Kurukshetra when the latter had lost his composure and forgotten his responsibilities after seeing his loved ones standing on the opposite side ready to fight him. The seven hundred and one verses of the Bhagavad Gita are believed to contain the nectar of the *Sanatana Dharma* (meaning "the Eternal Religion"), as documented in the Vedas, the oldest religious texts ever, penned by the author form of God Himself, Veda Vyasa.

Take it one topic at a time. Allow your mind to process what you've learned. I recommend that when you come across a new idea, you close your eyes, sit in silence, and meditate on it. Try to evaluate its worth. Do not dismiss any idea straightaway. Make a mental note of it and return to it in a few days. Everything will start to make sense, I promise.

I have one last request before we begin. Read the book till the very end or you may misinterpret quite a few of the points discussed herein.

Everything is linked. And to complete the puzzle you will need to join in *all* the pieces.

So, with all that in mind, let's dive into the Bhagavad Gita's divine pool of wisdom.

Day 1: Arjuna's Dilemma (Aren't We All Like Him?)

"I am also unable to stand firmly, and my mind seems to be rambling. I can only see adverse omens, O Keshava (Krishna)." [BG 1.30]

As described in the great epic Mahabharata, Dhritarashtra and Pandu were two brothers born in the ancient Kuru dynasty. Dhritarashtra was born blind, and so his younger brother Pandu inherited the throne. Pandu, however, died young. Dhritarashtra was then made the king. Pandu's sons (known as the Pandavas) were raised alongside the sons of Dhritarashtra (known as the Kauravas).

The two groups of cousins had a strained relationship. Dhritarashtra's sons, especially the eldest, Duryodhana, despised the virtuous Pandavas. The blind king was partial as well, swayed by his love for his own sons. Duryodhana even plotted to kill the Pandavas and their mother Kunti with the help of his maternal uncle Shakuni. However, the Pandavas were able to escape with the help of their cousin Krishna (who was Kunti's nephew).

Duryodhana then challenged Pandavas to a 'friendly' gambling match. Shakuni, a skilled gambler, cheated during the game, leading the Pandavas to lose everything, including their kingdom. The Pandavas were exiled for thirteen years. When the Pandavas returned from exile to claim their kingdom, Duryodhana retorted arrogantly that he would not give them enough land to stick a pin into.

War remained the only option for the Pandavas. Arjuna, the third of the Pandava brothers and the best archer in the world, and Duryodhana went to see Krishna and ask for his assistance. As fate would have it, they both left at the same time. Duryodhana was the first to arrive. Krishna was sound asleep at the time, and Duryodhana stood by His head, waiting for Him to awaken. Arjuna arrived a few minutes later and, seeing Krishna sleeping, reverently stood by His feet. Since Krishna first saw Arjuna when He awoke, much to Duryodhana's annoyance, custom dictated that Krishna should grant Arjuna's request first. He announced that one side could have His army and the other could have Him. He, however, made it clear that He would not take part in the upcoming war as a king or warrior. Duryodhana was aware of Krishna's vast military forces and was furious that Arjuna had been given the choice first. However, he was surprised and delighted when Arjuna chose Krishna over His military troops. Knowing Krishna's true identity,

Arjuna was content to have his Lord on his side, regardless of whether He fought or not. He requested Krishna to be his charioteer and guide in the great war, which Krishna pleasantly agreed to.

All armies assembled on the great battlefield of Kurukshetra. When the war was about to begin, Arjuna asked Krishna to draw up his chariot in between the two vast armies, so that he could see who all had gathered to fight in this great battle. As he surveyed both sides, he saw friends and family all around. Standing opposite him were his cousins, the sons of his uncle Dhritarashtra. Present also was his military teacher Drona, for whom he had a great deal of respect. The opposing armies were led by Bhishma, the great-grandsire of the Kuru dynasty, who had lavished love on all the Pandava princes, especially Arjuna. Bhishma had to take Duryodhana's side as he had pledged to remain a servant of the throne all his life. Arjuna then saw many other friends and relatives standing on both sides, ready to fight. Overcome by love and compassion for his loved ones, Arjuna slumped down on his chariot, and perplexed about the right course of action, asked Krishna to be his spiritual guide and to advise him.

He says to Krishna, "O Govinda, of what avail to us is dominion; of what avail is pleasure, or even life? The very ones for whom we desire kingdom, enjoyment and pleasure stand here in battle, having renounced life and wealth — teachers, fathers, sons, and also grandfathers, maternal uncles, fathers-in-law, grandsons, brothers-in-law, and other kinsmen. I do not wish to kill them, O Madhusudana, even though I may be killed by them, not even for the dominion over the three worlds, what to speak of the earth. What pleasure can we gain from killing the sons of Dhritarashtra, O Janardana? Sin alone with come upon us by slaying these felons." [BG 1.32-1.36]

Noticing Arjuna's bewilderment, Lord Krishna transforms into his spiritual master and sings to him His divine song, the Bhagavad Gita, enlightening him about the greatest truths in the universe and dispelling all his doubts and fears.

In those times, human society was divided into four classes according to the nature of work one was prescribed to perform. One of those classes was Kshatriya — the royal caste in charge of administering, preserving, and ensuring justice for the general public. A Kshatriya had the duty to fight for the right cause at all costs. And Arjuna was a Kshatriya of the highest order. However, he had lost track of who he was and thus wanted to give up fighting.

The question that arises now is: What was the reason for all this fear and confusion? Arjuna wished to reclaim his kingdom. And since the war was the only choice left for the Pandavas, he *had* to fight. The decision was already made after careful thought. What was the basis of this perplexity then? Was he afraid of losing and dying considering the massive opposing army, and was thus just making up excuses to not fight? Was he a coward? Or was he genuinely compassionate, which led to his uncertainty about whether or not to fight?

Arjuna was not a coward. That possibility is out of the question. If you have read the Mahabharata or have heard about Arjuna's character and abilities, you would know that he was of the bravest kind. He had won the greatest battles single-handedly. He had, in fact, defeated all the brave and able warriors who currently stood on his opposite side just a few weeks before the great war of Mahabharata, in the battle of Virata, all on his own, without any army.

However, the war that was about to begin was different — the biggest ever. And he needed to *kill* his loved ones to win it. They were the people he had spent his youth and adulthood with. They were his seniors and friends, whom he admired and adored. He couldn't bear the thought of injuring them, let alone attempting to murder them. Yes, he was aware that he would face them before entering the battleground. But seeing them face-to-face on the opposite side was a different thing altogether. He realized that they all would soon be dead. Compassion was the obvious response, which resulted in anxiety and perplexity.

We all have an Arjuna inside of us. We're all anxious. There is something or the other always itching the back of our brains. One who has money doesn't have time to enjoy it. One who has time has no money to enjoy it with. One who has both doesn't have genuine friends to speak to. There are diseases, worries, and pains. There are so many financial, relationship, and health issues to handle. Nobody is perfectly happy in this material world. One may seem to possess everything, but there is some piece of the puzzle of life that is always missing.

We are all confused as well, though we do not accept it for a fact. We have no idea where we have come from and where we need to go. We are just moving through the motions without a clear sense of direction. We have forgotten our Creator and our true home, and have lost sight of our purpose.

The source of our fear and perplexity is the impure thought pattern that this material world imposes upon us. This is why, upon seeing Arjuna shivering with anxiety, the Blessed Lord says, "O Arjuna, in this perilous condition, from where has this impure despondency come upon you, suitable only for unenlightened people, which brings dishonor, and does not lead to heaven?" [BG 2.2]

So if we are anxious and confused, what is the way out? Let's look at it tomorrow.

Key Takeaways

1. We are all perplexed and worried, though it may not always be evident.
2. The cause of our confusion and anxiety is our impure thinking pattern, which stems from material contamination.

Day 2: Discover Yourself Today

"But never indeed, I, at any time, did not exist, nor you, nor all these rulers of men; nor verily, will any of us ever cease to exist hereafter." [BG 2.12]

Have you ever had a dream in which you find yourself in an extremely stressful situation? For example, you see you have your university exam that day but can hardly recall your lessons, or you are stuck in traffic on the way to a crucial job interview, or worse your child has met with an accident and there is no hospital nearby. You are drenched in sweat. You are unable to think clearly. Your heart begins to beat like a drum. You are shivering and your nerves are getting the best of you. You have the feeling you're going to pass out.

What is the solution to these problems?

Well, all you have to do is *wake up!*

This is the *only* lasting solution to the challenges we all face in our lives — waking up.

But waking up to what? Waking up to our true identities. Waking up to the infinite knowledge about God contained in the authentic scriptures.

Waking up to our purpose. Waking up to truth and reality.

Today, let us focus on waking up to our true nature and discovering who we really are.

We normally identify ourselves with our bodies. But are we, in reality, our bodies? When you say "my body," you're implying that the 'body' you're referring to is yours. However, can you and something you *own* be the same? Only one thing can be deduced from this: you are not your body.

Then who *are* you? Your mind? Your brain? But again, it's *your* mind and *your* brain.

Let me ask you this: What makes us feel sad when we see a loved one dead? The body is still there, and it is possible to preserve it. Then what makes us want to cry? Why is the body not enough for us? What else do we need? What we need is a body with *life*. But then what is life? Life is the true identity of that person, not his physical form. Life is what defines him. If life isn't present, the individual is reduced to a mere object.

We take such good care of our bodies. To make our bodies look appealing to ourselves and others, we go to the gym, do yoga, and use sunscreens, fairness creams, and whatnot. This gives us a sense of importance, or in other words, it feeds our egos. But is the body actually attractive? Ask this to a surgeon. He will tell you the truth; because he has seen the 'beauty' of the body as it is — intestines, muscles, flesh, and bones, all surrounded by blood. It's not a pretty sight, believe me. But we do an amazing job of concealing it with colorful clothes, make-up, fancy hairstyles, and expensive perfumes. And then we forget about reality and are happy about it. We don't want to see ourselves beyond what is visible — our skin. We love the illusion. And therein lies the problem.

The single biggest cause of our suffering is that we do not know who we are and have no desire to learn.

I urge you to give this some really serious thought. In fact, I think this deserves to be written more explicitly —

YOU ARE NOT YOUR BODY.

But if you are not your body, then who really *are* you? I think this should be getting clearer by now. You are something beyond your body that lives within the body. You can call it spirit, self, or soul. I prefer to call it *soul*.

The word "spirituality" itself implies we are spirit souls. This makes it so obvious. But sadly, most of us still don't get it. Spirituality is nothing but seeking knowledge of the self — the spirit. But modern-day spirituality seems to have little to do with this quest. Today, spirituality has been reduced to a fancy method of relaxing and entertaining one's mind through meditations and mindfulness techniques. Meditation and mindfulness are excellent tools for mind-management and can help one get closer to one's true identity if practiced with that intention. However, simply practicing these techniques with no goal of discovering oneself is not spirituality.

Lord Krishna makes it very clear in the Bhagavad Gita when He says, "As boyhood, youth and old age are for the embodied (the soul) in this body, similar is the attainment of another body; this being so, a wise man is never bewildered seeing such changes." [BG 2.13]

He gives an easy-to-understand analogy to ensure we get this right. He says, "Just as a person, casting off worn-out clothes, puts on other new ones, in the same way, the embodied (the soul), relinquishing decayed bodies, verily accepts other new ones." [BG 2.22]

We often hear that "death is a great leveler." Actually, the biggest leveler is the fact that we are all souls. That is why, "The wise sages, endowed with knowledge and humility, look with an equal eye upon a Brahmin (a learned man of the highest class), a cow, an elephant, a dog (the different grades of lower creatures) and even an outcast (the lowest creature of all)." [BG 5.18] Self-realized sages hate nobody and harm nobody, as they know that, by nature, we are all the same. It's just our outer material bodies that make us *look* different.

Characteristics of a soul

In the Bhagavad Gita, Lord Krishna explains the various attributes of a soul in great detail.

The first characteristic of a soul is that it passes from one body to another. When a living being dies, the soul inside its body is released and it returns to Godhead, where it belongs. Then, depending on its previous karma, it is either given a new body and returned to the material world, or is freed from the cycle of births and deaths. If it is released from the cycle of births and deaths, it becomes a permanent resident of the *Bhagvat Dham*, or the Lord's home, called *Vaikuntha*. In the coming days, we'll learn more about God's Holy abode and the principle of karma.

If the soul is unable to achieve liberation from the continuous loop of births and deaths, it is reincarnated on this planet in a body based on its previous karma. According to the Vedic texts, there are 8,400,000 species of life and a soul may acquire a body in any of these. The body that it gets depends upon the mental tendencies of its previous body at the time of its death. So the new body may be that of a human, an animal, a bird, an insect, a fish, a tree, or any of the 8,400,000 different forms of life.

The second characteristic of a soul is its indestructibility. This is great news. If we are all souls, and the soul is indestructible, then we can safely draw one conclusion: WE CANNOT DIE. We are eternal beings. Of course, if we are born into the body of a dog or an insect, our lives would be difficult. And that is what the Bhagavad Gita attempts to assist us with — making the most of this one-of-a-kind human life and breaking free from this vicious cycle by better understanding ourselves, God, and our relationship with Him.

The other features of the soul related to its indestructible nature, as described by the Lord in the Bhagavad Gita, are listed below. According to the Bhagavad Gita, a soul:

- cannot be cut into pieces by any weapon,
- cannot be burned by fire,
- cannot be moistened by water,
- cannot be withered by the wind,
- is unbreakable, and
- is insoluble.

A soul's third major attribute is that it is all-pervasive. A soul has practically no shape and no size. Anything with a shape and size has limits and can only go as far as those limits allow.

Something that has no shape or size is unrestricted and can infiltrate everything. Therefore, even though the soul is tiny, it pervades the entire body and gives it life.

The fourth major characteristic of the soul is its changelessness and stability. A soul remains a soul and does not change its form ever. It is the body that it lives in that changes. But the soul never changes and always remains as it is.

The fifth significant attribute of the soul is that it is invisible to material eyes. As per the Svetasvatara Upanishad, "When the tip of a hair is divided into one hundred parts and each of these parts is further divided into one hundred parts, each of these parts is the measure of the dimension of the spirit soul." [SU 5.9] The human eye cannot see such a small object as a soul.

The sixth major feature of the soul is that it is inconceivable. How can something that moves from one body to another, is indestructible, all-pervading, changeless, and invisible, possibly be fully understood by us in our human form? Our intelligence and senses are both severely constrained. All we can get is a glimpse of what a soul really is. But that is enough for us to return to our actual home, where we can gain all the knowledge that cannot be acquired here. However, all souls are not that fortunate. That is why Krishna says, "Someone visualizes it (the soul) as a wonder; another, similarly indeed, speak of it as a wonder; and similarly, another hears of it as a wonder; and another, indeed, even after hearing about it, does not understand it." [BG 2.29]

But if we are all souls and we do not die, what is it we call "death?" We'll figure it out tomorrow.

Key Takeaways

1. The only lasting solution to all the suffering is to awaken to our true selves, to the knowledge about God, and to our life's purpose.
2. We are not our bodies. We are pure, unblemished souls.
3. The important characteristics of a soul are:
   a. it passes from one body to another,
   b. it cannot be destroyed,
   c. it is all-pervasive,
   d. it is changeless,
   e. it cannot be seen with material eyes, and
   f. it cannot be understood with material senses.

Day 3: On Death and Beyond

"It (the soul) never takes birth, nor it ever dies; it neither comes into being, nor it ever ceases to be. It is unborn, eternal, changeless, and primeval. It is not slain when the body is slain." [BG 2.20]

Before you can comprehend death, you must first recognize yourself as a soul. I believe you've already done that yesterday. You now have a clear understanding of who you are and who you are not. You are a soul — not a body, mind, or anything else — but a pure and flawless soul. And so is every other living being, be it an ant or an elephant, a microbe or a mosquito, a starfish or a shark, a jade plant or a banyan tree, a sparrow or an ostrich.

The next step is to understand the characteristics of the soul. You did this yesterday as well. And so, I believe, you already have a better understanding of death too. Today we will build upon this knowledge.

Understanding death is crucial for spiritual upliftment. You can become a master of your future, a master of death, and a master of yourself if you gain this knowledge. It will put an end to the greatest fear of all — the fear of death.

Let us consider what Krishna says about our true identity and death in His divine song.

Lord Krishna tells Arjuna, "The unreal (the body) has no existence; the real (the soul) has no nonexistence. Verily, the ultimate truth about both of these is realized by the seers of the truth (the realized sages). But know that to be indestructible by which all this (the entire body) is pervaded. No one can bring about the destruction of the imperishable (the soul)." [BG 2.16-2.17]

This proves that the soul — your actual personality and essence — is immortal. That means, as I said yesterday, you, I, and all other living beings are eternal. And so the Lord, after noticing Arjuna's perplexity and grief, says to him, "While you speak words of wisdom, you are grieving for those who are not to be grieved for. The wise mourn neither for the departed (dead) nor for the non-departed (living)." [BG 2.11]

Each of us has come to this planet for a very specific reason and for a very short period. And death is nothing more than a doorway through which we, the souls, pass from one body to another, whether it be material or spiritual. Death is not the end of the road. It's a fresh beginning.

In the coming days, we will try to understand the purpose of human lives. But there is one thing I would like to mention here. God would not have created us — the humans — without a purpose. He could not have taken the effort to make the most conscious of all living beings on earth just for the sake of it. But what if we are not able to fulfill that purpose in our current lifetimes? We would need to be disciplined and then given another opportunity. And this cycle would continue until the point we fulfill that purpose. What other way could it be? And the Vedic sciences completely support and confirm this notion. It all makes perfect sense.

We've all been born several times and have died several times. We may have not always lived as humans though. As you learned yesterday, according to the Vedic scriptures, there are 8,400,000 species of life. Human life is just one of them. And humans are the only species with the ability to advance spiritually. Before taking our human form, we may have lived as dogs, goats, or even mosquitoes. That is why our current human life is a very rare opportunity to accomplish our divine mission. Missing this opportunity invariably leads to the greatest loss ever, trapping us in this never-ending cycle once more.

Being eternal does not grant us the freedom to live our lives as we please. We have a clear goal to achieve (which we will look at in a few days). And it is *our* responsibility — our *sole* responsibility —

to achieve that goal. And, since our present bodies are impermanent, we only have a limited amount of time to achieve that goal. Because our bodies are transient, we must enquire about our actual mission in life and do everything we can to achieve it. The fact that we have a limited amount of time should motivate us to move quickly. Who knows when our time limit will be reached? This concept of impermanence is one of the pillars of Buddhism, which emphasizes keeping one's focus on attaining *Nirvana* without wasting a single moment. And the Bhagavad Gita and the other Vedic scriptures also stress this important point.

So we understand that we (humans and the other living beings) are all souls. And souls never take birth, and they never die, meaning we are immortal. We also understand that we enter a body and then quit that body to enter another body, and this cycle continues (till a certain point which we will understand in a few days). This implies that we can reincarnate in one of the 8,400,000 types of bodies. And the human body is only one of the many forms we can take, making this a very rare opportunity to advance spiritually.

But is there a way we can make death our best friend? Yes, there is. Lord Krishna says, "And whoever, in the last moments of his life, while quitting the body, goes forth remembering Me alone, attains My Being (by gaining oneness with

Krishna). There is no doubt about this." [BG 8.5] Want to become one with God? Remember Him while dying. It is, of course, not that straightforward. It requires the development and practice of a lot of virtues, which we will explore in the coming days. The state of one's mind at the time of death (which is a product of one's karma) is what decides his fate — whether he would take another birth in this material world, or would move to the spiritual world, or will go to the heavenly or hellish planets to negate his positive or negative karmas. (Don't worry if something looks confusing. Everything will become crystal clear by the time you reach the end of the book. That's a promise.)

The state of one's mind at the time of death is crucial, as it is the ultimate measure of one's spiritual knowledge and dedication. That is what determines whether one has fulfilled the purpose of his material life or not. And the time to prepare for it is now!

Key Takeaways

1. We are souls, and souls never take birth or die. This makes us immortal.
2. Death is a gateway for us, the souls, to move from one body to another, which may either be a material body or a spiritual one.

3. Reincarnation is an actual phenomenon, rather than a fictional myth.
4. We've all been born and died several times, and the cycle will continue until we reach our divine goal.
5. There are 8,400,000 species of life. The human form is just one of them. And our mental state at the time of death determines which form we take in the next life.
6. The fact is that the body dies. We cannot stay in human form indefinitely. And since the human form is the only material form capable of gaining spiritual knowledge and advancing spiritually, we must remember that we cannot afford to waste our limited time on material pleasures.

Day 4: Ego - the Enemy Within

"While all actions are actually carried out by the
attributes of material nature, one whose intelligence is
deluded by ego thinks, "I am the doer"." [BG 3.27]

Today we come to a very important point in our
quest for the Absolute Truth. And the point is: "Is
our ego worth it?"

We consider ourselves to be extremely
significant. We are the nucleus of the universe for
ourselves. We go to great lengths to ensure our
happiness. And we almost kill ourselves with
anxiety because we give too much importance to
incidents and situations that, in our opinion,
should be taken very seriously. But are we that
significant in the grand scheme of things? Let's
look at what our real position in the universe is.

On the 14th of February 1990, the Voyager 1
space probe took a photograph of the Earth from
a record distance of six billion kilometers. That
photograph gives us a whole new perspective of
our position in the universe. Our planet looks like
nothing more than a small dot in that
photograph. Renowned scientist Carl Sagan
wrote a bestselling book based on this

photograph titled *Pale Blue Dot: A Vision of the Human Future in Space*. In that book, he writes:

Look again at that dot. That's here. That's home. That's us. On it everyone you love, everyone you know, everyone you ever heard of, every human being who ever was, lived out their lives. The aggregate of our joy and suffering, thousands of confident religions, ideologies, and economic doctrines, every hunter and forager, every hero and coward, every creator and destroyer of civilization, every king and peasant, every young couple in love, every mother and father, hopeful child, inventor and explorer, every teacher of morals, every corrupt politician, every "superstar," every "supreme leader," every saint and sinner in the history of our species lived there — on a mote of dust suspended in a sunbeam.

That is what it means to put things in perspective. I strongly encourage you to look up 'pale blue dot image' on the internet and see it for yourself. You'll be astounded by how insignificant our physical existence is. Then come back and read Carl Sagan's words again, or read his book. If you've never considered things from that angle before, I guarantee it will be eye-opening.

Next, let's explore our (in)significance from the perspective of time. So how old are you? Twenty? Thirty? Sixty? Ninety? Science tells us our universe is a mind-numbing 13.8 billion years old. Our brains are not even developed enough to be able to think on that time scale. Moving closer, the age of our Earth is considered to be about 4.5

billion years. And the first forms of life are considered to have appeared about 4.2 billion years ago. And the first human, in the form we exist today, appeared about 200,000 years ago from the present times.

Now, if you live to be a hundred years old, what percentage of the total age of the universe would you be a member of at the end? It's far too small to be considered. If we consider the age of the world to be a movie, a human's age will just be a single frame of it — a frame that, if removed, will have absolutely no effect on the movie.

So our planet Earth, beyond which we never take our thoughts, has practically no significance when compared to the vastness of the entire creation. And our entire lifetimes, which we subconsciously believe to be endless, pale in comparison to the infinite stretches of eternity that expand before and after our existence.

So, are you the richest person on the planet? Are you the most powerful politician in the world? Are you the strongest person in the world? Are you the best athlete in the world? The most proficient accountant? The highest-earning lawyer? Do you hold or wish to hold world records? How fulfilling would it be to hold a world record now that we know our world is nothing more than a speck of sand in the vastness of the universe? How important do our lives seem in general after realizing that they bear no significance compared to the age of creation? We are practically non-existent.

However, this thought does not depress me in the least. It is, in fact, enlightening. It's a ticket to liberation, consciousness, knowledge, and truth. The first thing you become free of when you become conscious of your actual status is ego. You become more compassionate when you understand that everyone else's *physical* existence is as insignificant as your own.

But does this imply that you and your life have no significance at all? Certainly not. At this moment ask yourself how important *you* consider your life to be — but not in an egotistical way. If you realize the purpose of your life on earth, your life is important. If not, then also it's not lacking significance. It's still a part of the system that God has built. And what distinguishes us from all other creatures is that we have the ability to progress spiritually. That is why human life is so valuable. Human life is a blessing that should not be squandered.

In fact, when you combine this sense of insignificance with your spiritual truth, which scriptures like the Bhagavad Gita and Srimad Bhagavatam (also known as the Bhagavata Purana) can awaken you to, you will realize that although you are insignificant in terms of your material existence, you are not insignificant at all in terms of your spiritual nature. How can being part of the Absolute Truth be a small thing? So your task is to use this science-based 'insignificance' as a weapon to defeat your ego, which is the product of you placing too much value on your body and belongings, and then embark on a self-realization quest of rediscovering your true status.

Letting go of our egos is one of the most crucial steps in getting to know ourselves. We go to great lengths to feed our egos. Most of the work in our lives is done solely to appease our egos (although we don't always realize this). But actually, we don't need much to live a happy life. To live happily, we don't need a penthouse, a Ferrari, the best job title, a large bank account, the most attractive partner, or the nicest clothing. Yet we keep chasing these objects of pleasure all our lives. And then we die, either satisfied to have achieved these things or disheartened that we failed. And that is what most of us don't get. *We die.*

But where does this ego stem from? It is the most vicious result of us wrongly identifying with our bodies. We do not know who we are (souls) and we are proud of meaningless belongings which are actually the possessions of who we are not (material bodies). In reality, *nothing* belongs to us. And so we have nothing to be proud of in terms of material possessions. This is false ego. There is also a true ego — the ego that comes from the realization that we are all parts of the Supreme Being. True ego is pure. It is formed of love and devotion for the Lord. That is the kind of ego we should strive for.

Ego (false ego) is the most stubborn of all negative emotions, and it frequently sets off other nasty emotions such as rage, fear, and jealousy. It takes a lot of mental effort to get ego out of our heads. However, after you've let go of your ego, the feeling is great. You feel much lighter. You break away from the grasp of a master you were not even aware was your master up until now. You immediately begin to experience spiritual liberation. That is the reason Krishna says, "That person attains peace who, giving up all desires, moves about without longing, devoid of the ideas of 'I' (identifying himself with his mortal body) and 'mine' (material ownership)." [BG 2.71]

False ego does not allow you to accept the authority of anyone else (including God) and always wants you to believe that you are the center of the universe. Wayne Dyer says, "You can either be a host to God or a hostage to your ego. It's your call." This is why, before seeking spiritual enlightenment, it is crucial that you crush your ego.

Lord Krishna instructs in the Bhagavad Gita, "Having your consciousness fixed on Me, you will cross over all obstacles by My grace (and will ultimately reach Krishna); but if, out of ego, you do not listen to My teachings, you will be destroyed (by falling into the vicious cycle of birth and death)." [BG 18.58]

So ask yourself every day: What is the significance of my body in this boundless universe? What is the significance of my existence in the endless stretch of time? If I am not the body and do not actually own anything material, is there any logic in my pride? Will I be able to carry through what I consider mine, be it tangible (the big house, the expensive car, the gleaming jewelry) or intangible (the job title, the flattery, and praise from others), to the next life? If I can die any moment, isn't my false ego a sign of my short-sightedness, unconsciousness, and foolishness? Be honest in your responses. These responses may go a long way in making you more successful in your spiritual journey.

Key Takeaways

1. Among the trillions of planets and stars in the universe, our Earth has no relevance. As compared to the age of the universe, which is measured on trillion-year timescales, our entire lives are insignificant. In the grand scheme of things, we are practically non-existent.

2. The first thing you become free of when you become conscious of your status in the grand scheme of things is ego.
3. Though you are insignificant in terms of your material existence, you are not at all insignificant in terms of your spiritual nature.
4. False ego is the most damaging result of us wrongly identifying with our bodies, whereas true ego, being formed of love and devotion for the Lord, is pure.
5. False ego is the most stubborn of all negative emotions and often triggers other negative emotions like anger, fear, and envy.
6. Only an ego-free person can attain true and lasting peace of mind and spiritual enlightenment.

Day 5: Krishna - The Absolute Truth

"O Arjuna, I know all the beings of the past, the present, and the future; but Me no one knows." [BG 7.26]

People often ask me if I can tell them for certain whether or not there is a God. I refuse to give them the "yes" or "no" that they want. Rather, I simply ask them to put on their common-sense hats and see if they can sense a divine presence around them. I would encourage you to do the same. Look at nature and you will see a much greater power at work.

I discuss this at length in *Bhagavad Gita - The Perfect Philosophy*. Here's an excerpt for you:

Let us begin by looking at our own bodies. We have eyes to see, ears to hear, a mouth to eat and communicate with, a digestion system, a respiration system, a reproduction system, and a complex arrangement of cells on our skin to cover it all. How possible is it that such a grand design was built accidentally?

Consider the millions of species of life, the billions of galaxies in space, the sun that gives us light, the moon that keeps the night sky bright, the seasons, the rains, the mountains, the rivers, grass sprouting from the soil, a baby being born, our complex brains, our ability to think and make decisions — everything, tangible or intangible, clearly pointing to one thing — that there is a power much greater than we can comprehend that keeps this whole creation running.

Is it by chance that we have oxygen, water, food, and everything else we need to survive on this planet? How could the birds, animals, fishes, and insects have been created by accident? Is it just luck that gravity holds us anchored to the ground?

There is enough evidence around us to prove without a doubt that the universe is managed by a Supreme Being. God's presence is too obvious to ignore.

I've always been a big fan of nature and enjoy learning about the fascinating natural phenomena that most of us are oblivious to. What's more astounding is how pondering about these incredible facts can help us raise our consciousness levels. Nature has all the answers. So when in doubt, simply observe nature. As examples, consider these amazing facts about animals and birds:

- During the Arctic winter, a bird named arctic tern follows summer all the way to the Antarctic Circle on the other side of the planet, the shortest distance between the two being about 19,000 kilometers (12,000 miles). Because arctic terns do not fly in a straight line, their actual flight distance is even greater. According to Wikipedia, the average arctic tern travels over 2.4 million kilometers (1.5 million miles) over the course of its thirty-year lifespan, the equivalent of more than three round-trips from Earth to the Moon. I wonder what provides them with their sense of direction, as well as their strength and endurance. Accident?

- The hair of a polar bear is not white; it's colorless. It appears white because each of its hairs is hollow and reflects light. The skin behind the transparent fur is black, which absorbs heat from the sun and keeps the bear warm. Coincidence?

- Hummingbirds can beat their wings up to 200 times per second to hover. How is that even possible?

- It is fascinating how an egg transforms into a caterpillar which then sheds its skin several times to transform into a pupa (which appears to have no life), which then gives birth to a butterfly. Metamorphosis is the scientific term for such transformation. The organs of the caterpillar dissolve into a semi-liquid state to form a pupa. Nothing about a pupa indicates that the soup-like liquid it contains is about to give birth to a beautiful butterfly. Isn't it highly unlikely that such a complex multi-step procedure came about by chance?

We have no idea how creation started and what happened in that fraction of a second between when there was nothing and when there was something. Scientists say that the universe was created by a gigantic explosion and have termed it the Big Bang. If the Big Bang is the cause of the creation, what could have caused the Big Bang? And if there is something that caused the Big Bang, what is it that caused that something that caused the Big Bang? Was that something created by pure chance? It's all right there in front of us, waiting to be discovered. It is only a matter of how willing, open, curious, and analytical our minds are.

We looked at nature and realized that all of this magnificence could not be a fluke. Let's now have a look at the many things that we *believe* we created. We humans have invented a great deal, and we continue to do so every day. Automobiles, robots, artificial intelligence, spacecraft, skyscrapers, cellphones, and computers are all examples of technological advancements. It's almost as though we're gods.

But do you think any of these inventions would have been possible if there hadn't been some kind of supernatural force at work behind the scenes (it's alright if you don't want to call it "God" for the time being)? Is our intelligence the result of drinking some sort of enchanted potion? Who designed the brain that enables us to create? Let us see what Lord Krishna says about this in the Bhagavad Gita: "And I am seated in the hearts of all (as soul); from Me come memory, knowledge, as well as their loss; I am verily the one to be known through the study of the Vedas; indeed, I am the compiler of Vedanta (Upanishads), and I am the knower of the Vedas." [BG 15.15]

Another standpoint we can explore that would make the presence of God obvious is our sense of morality. We all know what is right and what is wrong. How we use this power is altogether a different matter. But that sense of morality could not result from a fluke. There must be a creator who bestowed this sense on us. Krishna, to support this view, declares, "Intelligence, knowledge, non-delusion, forgiveness, truthfulness, control of the senses, control of the mind, happiness, sorrow, birth, death, fear, and also fearlessness, non-injury (to the innocent), equanimity, contentment, austerity, charity, fame, infamy — all these various attributes of beings arise from Me alone." [BG 10.4-10.5]

For the benefit of all humanity, Lord Krishna reveals in the Bhagavad Gita, "(I am) the goal, the maintainer, the Lord, the witness, the abode, the refuge, the dearest friend, the origin, the annihilation, the foundation, the treasure-house, and the imperishable seed." [BG 9.18] Many more verses in the Bhagavad Gita explain the Lord's attributes, helping students of this scripture to become enlightened about the Supreme Person.

And once Arjuna gets disillusioned and becomes conscious of the potencies of the Supreme Lord, he says, "You are the father of the world — of the moving and the nonmoving; You are also its glorious preceptor, worthy of worship. There is no one equal to You; then how can there be anyone superior to You in the three worlds, O Lord of unequalled power?" [BG 11.43]

If you wish to learn more about Lord Krishna, Srimad Bhagavatam is the best guide for you. It details the Lord's different pastimes and describes His nature and personality. It's pretty long though — over 14,000 verses (when translated into English) divided into 12 cantos. However, it is so captivating that a genuine devotee will not find it long at all.

Vedic science informs us that Krishna is the "cause of all causes." The very first verse of Srimad Bhagavatam says, "I meditate upon Lord Krishna because He is the Absolute Truth and the cause of all causes of the creation, maintenance, and destruction of the universe. He is all-conscious, and He is not bound as there is no other cause beyond Him." [SB 1.1.1 (excerpt)]

Let us look at a verse from Brahma Samhita as well. "Krishna, also known as Govinda, is the Supreme Person. He has an ever-lasting, blissful spiritual body. He is the origin of everything, and He has no origin or cause." [BS 5.1]

Krishna is God — the Absolute Truth. We will reestablish this reality in the coming days through a more thorough examination of His various manifestations, the form in which He should be worshipped, His holy abode, and why we can't see Him with our naked eyes, as well as what we must do to see Him.

Key Takeaways

1. To determine whether there is a God, you can analyze nature with an open mind.
2. Once you acknowledge the existence of God, you must become curious to know who God is.
3. Krishna is the Absolute Truth, the Supreme Person, the Primeval Lord.

Day 6: Krishna - His Cosmic Form

"O Gudakesha (Arjuna), behold in My body the entire universe together at the same place, including the moving and the non-moving, and whatever else you wish to see." [BG 11.7]

On the battlefield of Kurukshetra, to show Arjuna the futility of his anxiety, Lord Krishna reveals His all-encompassing cosmic form. Lord Krishna's cosmic form is described vividly in the eleventh chapter of the Bhagavad Gita.

When, with the help of the divine knowledge shared by Lord Krishna, Arjuna is able to regain some of his composure, he requests the Lord thus: "O Lotus-eyed One, I have verily heard from You in detail about the appearance and disappearance of all beings, and also Your limitless glories. O Supreme Lord! As You have thus spoken about Yourself, I wish to behold Your divine form, O Purushuttama (the Supreme Person). If You think, O Lord, that it is possible to be seen by me, O Lord of Yoga, then kindly show me Your eternal Self." [BG 11.2-11.4]

The Lord replies, "Behold, O Partha (Arjuna), hundreds and thousands of My varied forms — divine, and of various colors and shapes." [BG 11.5]

The Lord then grants Arjuna divine eyes so that he can behold His universal cosmic form.

I represent the description of God's actual form as revealed in the Bhagavad Gita in *Bhagavad Gita - The Perfect Philosophy* as this:

The Bhagavad Gita describes the universal form of Krishna as having numerous mouths and eyes and numerous wonderful sights, wearing numerous divine ornaments, uplifting numerous divine weapons, wearing celestial garlands and apparel, anointed with divine scents — a body all-wonderful, brilliant, unlimited, facing all sides. If thousands of suns were to shine all at once in the sky, that might equal the radiance emanating from that great soul. Arjuna could see in that form many arms, bellies, mouths and eyes, thighs and feet, and the expanded forms did not have any beginning, middle, or end. The form is described to be adorned with various crowns, clubs, and discs, with the sun and the moon as its eyes and blazing fire coming from its mouths, heating the entire universe with its radiance. This form is said to be pervading the entire universe — giving birth to everything and also annihilating everything.

Such is the authentic form of the One who creates everything, contains everything, is everything, and yet stays untouched from everything. This is

Krishna. This is God. Who else can claim to be God — the Absolute Truth? Arjuna, thrilled with admiration after viewing Krishna's amazing cosmic form, exclaims, "You are the primal God, the oldest person; You are the supreme refuge of this universe. You are the knower, the knowable (the only one worthy of being known), and the supreme abode. O being of unlimited forms, the universe is pervaded by You!" [BG 11.38]

He goes on to say, "Salutation to You from the front and from behind; Salutation to You from all sides indeed, O Everything; You are infinite in power, infinite in prowess; You pervade everything; therefore, You are everything." [BG 11.40]

These words of Arjuna are extremely important and should be remembered at all times by anyone seeking spiritual growth in this life. There is no spirituality without the spirit, and there is no spirit without the spirit-creator, Lord Krishna, who is all-pervading. All those who thought of Lord Krishna as a poor cowherd were proven wrong in the Mahabharata. His uncle Kansa tried multiple times to kill Him (when He was a child), but was ultimately defeated. Those who refuse to acknowledge Krishna's supremacy because of their egos or biases are clearly mistaken. The Bhagavad Gita and the other Vedic texts make this extremely clear.

Realizing Krishna as the Supreme is enough to cleanse one's mind of all delusions. It has the power to dispel all fears, doubts, and rage. This knowledge about Krishna is eye-opening. It can make us instantaneously more caring and happy. If someone has any reservations regarding Krishna's authority, Krishna has a message for them as well. He says, "However, one who is ignorant and faithless, and has a doubting mind perishes (in his spiritual endeavors). For a person of doubting mind, there is neither this world, nor the next, nor bliss." [BG 4.40] On the other hand, "Whosoever, being undeluded, thus knows Me as Purushuttama (the Supreme Person), he, the all-knowing, worships Me with his whole being, O descendant of Bharata (Arjuna)." [BG 15.19]

Do not, however, misunderstand Krishna as an egoistic God who constantly brags about His powers. If one thinks at a superficial level, he would undoubtedly infer that Krishna is a con artist who preys on simpletons who fall for His alluring nature and blindly submit to Him. However, this is not so. In the Bhagavad Gita, He reveals His form and powers to us just to make us aware of the truth *as it is*. Otherwise, Lord Brahma, in the Brahma Samhita, would not have called Krishna the Supreme God having an eternal and blissful body, being the origin of everything, while having no origin Himself. Also, Arjuna, after seeing the Universal form of

Krishna, would not have called Him the "God of gods" in verse 11.37 of the Bhagavad Gita.

Today, let us realize that Krishna is God. Krishna is everything.

Key Takeaways

1. Krishna is the Supreme Lord. No one is above Him or equal to Him.
2. Realizing Krishna as the Supreme is enough to clear one's mind of all illusions. It has the power to dispel all fears, uncertainties, and wrath. This knowledge is enlightening.
3. Never doubt Krishna's sovereignty. If you have any reservations, read the Vedic scriptures to dispel them. Do it as if your life depends on it (because it actually does).

Day 7: God - Person? Power? Energy?

"Arjuna asked: Those devotees who, thus being ever engaged, worship You (Krishna's personal form), and also those who worship the imperishable and unmanifest (Krishna's impersonal form) — which of them are better versed in Yoga?" [BG 12.1]

This is an issue that most seekers struggle with. Is God a being or a force? Does God have a physical form or is He formless? This is a good query, and it suggests that the person making it is interested in knowing more about God.

Is the answer, however, not obvious? Isn't it true that God can take whatever form He wants? Isn't it possible for God to live in different forms at different times in different places? There is nothing impossible for the Almighty, or He would not be the Almighty. So God is both *Saguna* (with a physical form) and *Nirguna* (with no physical form). This is quite self-evident and, in my opinion, does not necessitate much debate.

But then there's another issue. In which form should a devotee think about and worship the Lord? Arjuna had the good fortune to ask this directly to Lord Krishna. And the Lord replied, "Those who, fixing their minds on Me, worship Me (Krishna's personal form), ever steadfast, endowed with great faith, are considered by Me to be the most perfect in Yoga. But those who fully worship the imperishable, the indefinable, the unmanifest, the all-pervading, the inconceivable, and the changeless, the immovable, the constant, by disciplining all the senses, being even-minded everywhere, engaged in the welfare of all beings, they also verily attain Me. Trouble is much greater for those whose minds are attached to the unmanifested (Krishna's impersonal form); for, the goal, the unmanifest, is difficult to be attained for the embodied soul." [BG 12.2-12.5]

Whether or not God looks like a human has long been a subject of discussion and debate among spiritualists and religious leaders. Is God a being or a force? Is God formless, or does He have a body? Can we see Him as we see each other, or His presence can only be experienced?

Lord Krishna clearly states that a devotee is free to choose the form in which he wants to worship Him. He can worship the Lord's form of Krishna or Vishnu, or he can choose to worship His formless features. He can also worship the Lord as His incarnations, such as Rama or Narsimha. But Krishna provides His valuable advice too. He advises the devotees to consider worshipping

Him *with* a form rather than without a form. The reason is easy to understand.

We are human beings, and though we are parts and parcels of the Almighty Lord, our mental abilities are limited because of the material nature of our bodies. We find it difficult to envision something or someone that does not have a physical body because of our mind's limited capacity. What abstract image of God can we conjure in our minds? Is it made of smoke? Is it a cloud? It's far too difficult to see God in this way. It's also not needed. We can easily picture Lord Krishna as a normal human being and worship Him. Of course, we must keep in mind that He is all-powerful, all-knowledgeable, all-beautiful, and all-mystical. But this method is obviously easier.

The biggest benefit of this method is that Lord's form as Krishna is all blissful and beautiful, which makes loving Him much easier and more satisfying. God, in His Krishna form, looks very pleasant, and visualizing Him in that form and worshipping His idol in that form is thus very easy for a devotee. The love for such a form flows quite naturally in our minds.

There are various known and unknown forms in which we can worship Krishna. Some of them are Rama, Krishna, Vishnu, Narsimha, Vamana, Chaitanya, Matsya, Varaha, and so on.

Then there's the Lord's dreadful cosmic form, which, though helps us understand Him and His powers and greatness, prevents us from falling in love with Him. Even Arjuna, a devout follower of the Lord, was terrified when he saw the Lord in His celestial form and requested that He appear in His human, Krishna-like form.

Thus, the form of the Lord that is easiest to adore and worship is clearly His Krishna form. One can easily keep chanting Krishna's name all day long, always thinking of this beautiful and transcendental form of His. It just makes the process of *Bhakti* (pure devotion to the Lord) so much easier.

One of the greatest Vaishnava (devotees of Lord Krishna) saints, Rupa Goswami (1489-1564 CE), enumerated as many as 64 unique attributes of Lord Krishna described in Vedic literature. If you wish to learn about Krishna, His pastimes, His different forms, His likes and dislikes, His personality, and everything else about Him, I highly recommend reading Srimad Bhagavatam. Veda Vyasa mentions everything about Krishna in the 14,000 verses of Srimad Bhagavatam. If you read Srimad Bhagavatam, you will learn about the Lord from the highest authority — Veda Vyasa, the Lord's author-form.

All that God expects from us is pure love for Him. This love, however, is not the typical romanticized love; it is pure, transcendental, and unconditional. There is no give-and-take involved. That love is solely the product of a devotee's understanding of Krishna's truth. In the entire universe, this is the purest kind of love.

Key Takeaways

1. Krishna is not restricted to a particular form. So we should not really be concerned about His actual form (although it is revealed clearly in the Bhagavad Gita as His cosmic form). What we should be concerned about is which of His forms we should worship.
2. Krishna's impersonal form is very difficult for a devotee to love. Worshiping Krishna in His personal form is a much more convenient and practical mode of worship.

Day 8: One God? Many Gods?

"Even the devotees of other gods, who worship them
with faith, they worship Me only, O Kaunteya
(Arjuna), though following the wrong method." [BG
9.23]

This has long been a point of contention among
spiritual seekers. Is there only one all-powerful
God, or are there many gods, each with their own
set of devotees? If you read the Bhagavad Gita,
Srimad Bhagavatam, and the other Vedic texts,
all of your questions about this issue will vanish
for good.

The quick answer to the question is: KRISHNA IS
THE SUPREME OF ALL BEINGS.

I had my doubts regarding this, as you may be
having at this point. If Krishna is the Supreme
Being, what about the other gods such as Shiva,
Ganesha, Hanuman, Rama, Durga, Laksmi, and
so many others? Vedic literature, especially the
Gita and the Bhagavatam, clearly answers this
question and establishes beyond a shadow of a
doubt that Krishna is the supreme force ruling
over all else. The other gods are either different
forms of Krishna or are demigods. We can

understand the demigods as the departmental heads of Krishna's kingdom. Here are a few verses from the Bhagavad Gita that will help you understand Krishna's supremacy over all other beings:

"Although I am unborn, am of imperishable nature, and am the Lord of all beings, yet, subjugating My own divine nature, I incarnate by My own nature (in Krishna's own way — not like a human takes birth normally)." [BG 4.6]

"There is nothing whatsoever superior to Me, O Dhananjaya (Arjuna). All things (beings and objects) are strung in Me, as a row of gems on a thread." [BG 7.7]

"I, in My unmanifested form, pervade this entire universe; all beings exist in Me, but I (Krishna's all-powerful Self) am not situated in them." [BG 9.4]

"He who knows Me as the unborn and the beginningless, and also as the Supreme Lord of all the worlds — he, among the mortals, is non-deluded, and is liberated from all sins." [BG 10.3]

Vedic literature is replete with such information that explains the identity of the Supreme Lord. But since the Bhagavad Gita summarizes those millions of verses in a way that makes it easy for us who, being born in *Kaliyuga*, neither have the time nor inclination to go through long texts, we can rely on the Gita to get most of our queries resolved.

Incarnations of Krishna

There have been many incarnations of the Supreme Being, as stated in Srimad Bhagavatam: "O Brahmanas, the incarnations of the Lord are numerous, like rivulets flowing from infinite sources of water." [SB 1.3.26]

However, out of all the various incarnations of the Supreme, Srimad Bhagavatam's verse 1.3.28 specifically states, "Lord Sri Krishna is the original Supreme Person." All others are His incarnations or *avatars*, who come to earth to perform specific tasks. Matsya, Kurma, Varaha, Narsimha, Vamana, Parshurama, Rama, and Balarama are just a few of Krishna's many incarnations.

The interesting thing to note is that there is one incarnation of Lord Krishna which is yet to take birth. His name is Kalki. Srimad Bhagavatam has given a good amount of clarity about the prophecy of the appearance of Lord Kalki:

"At the end of the Kaliyuga, when there would be no Godly subjects, except in the homes of so-called sages and decent men of the higher castes, and when the power of government would be transferred to ministers elected from the lower castes, and when no one would know how to make sacrifices, the Lord will appear as the ultimate chastiser." [SB 2.7.38]

"Lord Kalki will appear in the home of the great spirit, Vishnuyasha, the Shambhala village's most revered Brahmana." [SB 12.2.18]

The Vishnu Purana (Book 4, Chapter 24) also explains: "A portion of that Supreme Being who exists in His own divine nature, who is the root and end of all, and who comprehends all things, will descend upon this world when the rituals taught in the Vedas and institutions of law have nearly vanquished, and the end of the Kaliyuga approaches. Kalki, endowed with eight superhuman abilities, will be born into the family of Vishnuyasha, an eminent Brahmana of the Shambhala village."

We can find similar references in the Mahabharata, Agni Purana, Padma Purana, and Brahma-Vaivarta Purana, among other Vedic texts.

Who are demigods?

Krishna is all-merciful. He does not deny a devotee what he desires, works for, and to which he is entitled. Of course, He expects Himself to be the only wish a devotee should have. However, He recognizes that not all souls are blessed with the ability to nurture that desire and become free of materialistic urges. If that were the case, there would not have been a need to send them to this material world in the first place. That is the reason He has created various departments and has assigned their responsibilities to the appointed departmental heads. Below is an excerpt from *Bhagavad Gita - The Perfect Philosophy* related to this subject:

The concept of demigods is rather straightforward. Krishna appoints demigods and assigns them specific departments to manage, much like a government has multiple departments that handle the different and critical responsibilities required to run a country efficiently. This might look to be an oversimplification, but there is no better way to comprehend the relationship between Krishna and the demigods.

However, Krishna did not create demigods solely for the sake of keeping the universe functioning smoothly. That is something He could do Himself. The true goal is to test the *priorities* of seekers. For example, Goddess Laksmi is worshipped by those who value wealth above Krishna's association, Goddess Saraswati is worshipped by those who prefer gaining material knowledge to Krishna's love, Lord Hanuman is worshipped by those who desire power and protection more than Krishna's blessings, and so on. However, one who has no desire for material objects and simply craves the Lord's company will only worship Krishna with a pure heart, knowing Him to be the Absolute Truth. And only such a devotee is considered a first-class devotee in Krishna's eyes deserving of His love and attention.

That is why Krishna says in the Bhagavad Gita, "Desiring the fruits of their actions here, they (human beings) worship the demigods by making sacrifices; for material success is achieved quickly through result-oriented work in this mortal world." [BG 4.12]

But He adds, "Even the devotees of other gods, who worship them with faith, they worship Me only, O Kaunteya (Arjuna), though following the wrong method." [BG 9.23]

Krishna makes it very clear that the highest desire for a human is the desire for Krishna's association. One who is in perfect consciousness would never allow any desire of material sense pleasure to enter his mind and contaminate its pure nature. As we would see in the coming days, the desire for objects of sense gratification is one of the greatest impediments on the road to true spiritual advancement.

But most of us don't get it, and the Lord knows that. Most of us regard sense enjoyment as the sole purpose of human lives. And they subconsciously think of God as a continuous supplier of objects of pleasure. They are clearly deluded. But as Krishna is merciful, He fulfills their material desires through the demigods, who are nothing but His own material manifestations.

However, these department heads should not be confused as being the same as or equal to the Supreme Lord Krishna. He makes it amply clear that though the worshippers of the demigods worship Him only, it is not the ideal way to worship Him, as it involves the presence of material desires.

Krishna further goes on to say, "The devotees of the demigods go to the demigods; the devotees of the ancestors go to the ancestors; the devotees of the ghosts go to the ghosts; but My devotees come to Me." [BG 9.25]

Again, He confirms that if one wants His association, one needs to worship Him directly, and not through any of the demigods. This clearly tests the intentions and preferences of a devotee. A perfect yogi would never desire objects for His own pleasures. He would prefer being a servant of the Lord to all the wealth in all the worlds combined. And the knowledge that he would have gained about the importance of human lives and statuses of Lord Krishna, His incarnations, and the demigods would enable him to be firm in his stance. It would, in fact, be a straightforward choice for him.

And if someone still doubts Krishna's authority over the demigods, the Lord clarifies, "Neither the hosts of demigods nor the great sages know My origin; for in every way, I am the origin of the demigods and the great sages." [BG 10.2]

In the Bhagavad Gita, Lord Krishna reveals that He is superior to all demigods because He is the source of all demigods. This provides students of the Bhagavad Gita a significant advantage in achieving spiritual success by worshipping the original source of everything rather than worshipping a deity of their desires without adequate knowledge.

Thus, Arjuna, upon realizing the authority of the Lord, says, "I accept as truth all that You have told me, O Keshava (Krishna). Verily, neither the gods nor the demons, O Lord, can understand Your personality." [BG 10.14]

I hope, like Arjuna, you now have a firm grasp on the fact that Krishna is the Supreme One and the only One truly deserving of worship.

Key Takeaways

1. The desire for Krishna's association is the highest and purest desire of all. But this is

difficult to understand for most of us because of our material tendencies.

2. Lord Krishna has many manifestations, but He remains the source of each of them and thus the original Supreme Being.

3. To fulfill the material desires of deluded souls, Lord Krishna has appointed various department heads or demigods. One desiring a particular kind of material pleasure can worship the god of that desire.

4. It is important to realize that demigods should never be considered equal to Krishna. Krishna is the source of all and everything, including demigods. He is the only Supreme Person and the sole object of unconditional and pure worship.

Day 9: God's Abode and the Eternal Cosmos

"Having attained Me, the great souls, having reached the highest perfection, never take birth again in the temporary place full of miseries (the material world)."
[BG 8.15]

Where does God live? The quick answer to this question is, "It depends." "On what?" you may ask. The answer to this would be, "It depends on the form you are thinking about God (Krishna) in."

Let me elaborate. If you consider Krishna in His impersonal form, or no-form, you can deduce that He is everywhere and within everything. The Bhagavad Gita confirms this in verse 12.3. This 'everywhere' would include your heart as well. You can appreciate how easily God is accessible to those who are devoted to Him.

But what if you prefer to think of Krishna in His personal form? If He is a person, then He must be having a home. Of course, He has a home. And that home is called *Vaikuntha*. In Sanskrit, *vai* means "without," and *kuntha* means "anxiety." So Vaikuntha means "without anxiety." On the other hand, the material planet that we live on is called *kunthalok* — a place full of anxieties and miseries. The home of the Lord is free of worries and anxieties because everyone who lives there is fully conscious. They are all realized souls. There is no ignorance there. This is the purest place in the whole creation — untouched by any material whims and desires.

The third chapter of Srimad Bhagavatam includes a vivid description of Vaikuntha. It describes Vaikuntha as follows:

"There are many forests on those Vaikuntha planets that are very auspicious. The trees in those forests are wish-fulfilling and are full of flowers and fruits at all times of the year because everything in the Vaikuntha planets is spiritual and sacred.

The inhabitants of the Vaikuntha planets, accompanied by their wives and consorts, fly in their airplanes and sing endlessly of the Lord's character and activities, which are devoid of all inauspicious qualities. While singing the praises of the Lord, they mock even the blossoming *madhavi* flowers, which are full of fragrance and laden with honey.

The pigeon, the cuckoo, the crane, the *cakravaka*, the swan, the parrot, the partridge, and the peacock all have a temporary lull in their noise when the king of bees hums in a high pitch, singing the Lord's glories. Such transcendental birds pause in their singing simply to listen to the Lord's majesty.

While flowering plants such as the *mandara, kunda, kurabaka, utpala, campaka, arna, punnaga, nagakeshara, bakula*, lily, and *parijata* have transcendental fragrance, they are still aware of Tulasi's austerities, since the Lord favors Tulasi and garlands Himself with Tulasi leaves.

Vaikuntha's residents fly in lapis lazuli, emerald, and gold-encrusted planes. Their consorts' mirth and stunning charms do not arouse the male inhabitants to love, even though they have broad hips and beautiful smiling faces. The Vaikuntha planets' ladies are as breathtaking as the goddess of fortune herself. Such transcendentally beautiful ladies are often seen sweeping the marble walls, which are bedecked at intervals with golden borders, to get the grace of the Supreme Lord, their hands playing with lotuses and their leg bangles tinkling.

The goddesses of wealth offer Tulasi leaves on the coral-paved banks of transcendental pools of water to worship the Lord in their own gardens. They can see their beautiful faces with raised noses reflected in the water when offering worship to the Lord, and it appears that they have become more beautiful because of the Lord kissing their faces. Regrettably, unfortunate people do not discuss the Vaikuntha planets' descriptions." [SB 3.15.16-3.15.23]

Vaikuntha may appear to be a place straight out of a fairy tale. And you may be tempted to believe that such a place does not exist and that Vedic literature is nothing more than ancient science fiction. But isn't it obvious that a God who is pure and blissful will have a home such as this? Such features are very much expected to be present in His abode. So, there is no reason to question Vaikuntha's existence.

Wouldn't it be wonderful to live on such a planet? Who wouldn't want that? Vaikuntha is a realm devoid of desire. There is no desire there because there is no need for it. Conscious beings are free from material desires, and the highest spiritual desire, which is to live with Krishna and serve Him forever, is already fulfilled there. As the soul lives under the Lord's personal care and affection, it becomes one with Him. This is a place filled with everlasting joy and peace.

Only the purest souls have the chance to enter Vaikuntha — souls who are completely enlightened and sinless, souls who have no ambition other than to serve Krishna. And such souls do not return to the mortal world once they reach this perfect state of being. Krishna declares in the Bhagavad Gita, "Neither the sun illuminates that, nor the moon, nor fire, reaching which they (the liberated souls) do not return (to this mundane material world); that is My supreme abode." [BG 15.6] In verse 6.5.13 of Srimad Bhagavatam, it is again confirmed that once a soul reaches the spiritual world, it does not return to the material world.

In Vaikuntha, everybody is situated in transcendental bliss. This is confirmed in verse

1.1.12 of the Vedanta Sutra. Everybody is always joyful there. This is because that joy is not sourced from some impure object of material sense pleasure. The source of this joy is Lord Krishna — the source of everything. And Krishna is all-blissful. And so the place where He lives has to be all-blissful as well.

The truth about heaven and hell

The concept of *Swarga* (heaven) is based on a man's desire for material gratification.

Swarga, however, is not the same as Vaikuntha. It's a place where a soul can get some of its material desires fulfilled as a reward for being a good soul. That is everything there is to it. It's a place of reward, similar to when you enter a contest and win a trip to your dream holiday destination. The Lord rewards the soul with a temporary stay in *Swarga* for doing some humanitarian or other kinds of work that positively impacts the world in some way, or for making some sacrifices with a desire for material pleasures. Just the opposite of *Swarga* is *Narka* (or hell). It is a place where heinous souls go to be punished for their horrible deeds in the physical world. However, *Swarga* and *Narka* are not the soul's final destinations. After the time of pleasure or punishment has ended, the soul is returned to the mortal world to repeat the cycle of birth and death. Verse 9.21 of the Bhagavad Gita confirms this.

So heaven, as opposed to common knowledge, is not the abode of God. Vaikuntha is where Krishna lives and this is confirmed in the Vedic scriptures.

Seeing beyond the visible

Now you may ask, "Then where exactly is Vaikuntha?" Let's try to understand this with the help of Vedic cosmology.

There are trillions of universes in the whole of creation, of which our universe is only an insignificant part. Each universe comprises trillions of planets that are divided into three categories:

- *urdhva-loka* (upper planets) — comprising heavenly planets, the highest of which is *Brahma-Loka*
- *madhya-lok*a (middle planets) — comprising material (earthlike) planets
- *adho-loka* (lower planets) — comprising hellish planets, the lowest of which is *Patala-Loka*

All these planets in all the universes put together make one-fourth of the total creation. The remaining three-fourths comprise the spiritual world where the Vaikuntha planets are situated. Thus, heavenly planets are part of the material creation whereas the Vaikuntha planets are completely divine and exist in the spiritual sky.

Let us now see what Lord Krishna says about this in the Bhagavad Gita: "Those who know the day of Brahma (Lord's creator form), which runs for a thousand ages, and the night, which also runs for a thousand ages, they truly know 'day' and 'night.' At the coming of day, all beings become manifest from the unmanifest state; and at the coming of night they dissolve verily into what is called the unmanifest. Being born again and again, O Partha (Arjuna), the same throng of beings are annihilated (into the unmanifest state), helplessly, at the coming of night; and they again manifest at the coming of day. But there exists another Unmanifested nature (Krishna's divine home), transcendental to that unmanifested nature (where soul's go after annihilation of body before returning to the mortal world), which is eternal, and is not annihilated when the manifested nature (mortal world) is annihilated (into the unmanifested nature). That which is said to be the Unmanifested nature, the imperishable, is thus known as the highest goal, reaching which, one never returns. That is My supreme abode." [BG 8.17-8.21]

One day of Lord Brahma comprises a thousand cycles of the four *yugas* (or ages): Satya, Treta, Dvapara, and Kali. The Satya-Yuga is characterized by goodness and religion and lasts 1,728,000 years. In the Treta-Yuga, vice is introduced and continues to rise in the Dvapara-Yuga. These yugas last 1,296,000 and 864,000 years, respectively. In Kali-Yuga (the age we are living in) the ignorance of religion and prevalence of strife reaches its peak and it lasts 432,000 years. Brahma lives one hundred of such years, each day of which comprises one thousand cycles of the four yugas, and then dies. Brahma's age, by such calculations, comes to 311 trillion and 40 billion years. Material life appears at the dawn of each day of Brahma's life and dissolves again at dusk, and the cycle continues.

All this may look unbelievable to us, but in the grand scheme of things, it is not much. This is how the universe actually works. It is important for us to realize our role in this eternity. To put it simply, our ultimate life goal should be to reach the Vaikuntha planets rather than the heavenly planets. This is the only sustainable solution to all the miseries of material existence.

Key Takeaways

1. In His impersonal form, Krishna lives within the hearts of each of us.

2. In His personal form, Krishna lives in *Vaikuntha,* the most wonderful and blissful planet in the entire creation.

3. Only the purest devotees of the Lord can enter Vaikuntha, and entering it to serve the Lord is the supreme goal.

4. Swarga (Heaven) and Narka (Hell) are not where God lives. These are temporary places where souls are taken to negate the effects of their good and bad karma in their material lives.

Day 10: Modes of Material Nature

"Whichever forms of material life originate in all the wombs, O Kaunteya (Arjuna), the great Brahma is their true womb, and I am the seed-giving father." [BG 14.4]

The Lord has made every effort to make us realize that He is the Creator of all forms of life. And we have already discussed this at length.

However, we are yet to bring the mother into the picture (if there is a Father there has to be a mother, at least in the material world). Mother nature (material nature), created by Brahma, is what gives us our material bodies. This is confirmed by Krishna in verse 14.4 of the Bhagavad Gita.

The effect of mother nature giving us birth is that it also transforms its three primary modes or qualities to us in varying proportions. Krishna explains that there are three primary modes of material nature —

1. *sattva* (purity),
2. *rajas* (passion), and
3. *tamas* (darkness).

Let us understand what these modes of material nature are.

"Of these (three modes of material nature), the mode of purity, being immaculate, is illuminating and harmless. It however binds (the soul to the material world) through attachment to material happiness and attachment to knowledge, O Anagha (sinless Arjuna)." [BG 14.6]

"Know the mode of passion to be of the nature of ecstasy born of lust and attachment. O Kaunteya (Arjuna), it binds (the soul to the material world) through attachment to action (carried out with the objective of sense satisfaction)." [BG 14.7]

"But know the mode of darkness to be born of ignorance, which deludes all embodied beings. O descendant of Bharata, it binds (the soul to the material world) through heedlessness, laziness, and sleep." [BG 14.8]

Lord Krishna explains that the three modes of material nature are constantly battling for dominance over a person's mind. The mode of purity wants one to be attached to happiness and knowledge, the mode of passion wants him to be attached to artifacts of sense fulfillment, and the mode of darkness wants him to be attached to ignorance, indifference, and laziness.

We can see here that the mode of purity is the best of the three (obviously) and it is only by being in this mode and developing this quality can one expect to become spiritually informed and materially free. We can only achieve this mode through knowledge — pure spiritual knowledge (that is contained in Vedic scriptures, including the Bhagavad Gita). When one understands the true nature of the self, the truth about God, the truth about his divine purpose, and how material and spiritual natures work, he cannot help but develop a sense of purity. That change can be easily seen in the way he lives, his priorities, his daily routine, the way he behaves, and the way he goes through his daily activities. Everything such an individual does exudes a sense of purity.

As the name implies, the mode of passion is characterized by relentless hard work aimed at accumulating wealth in order to satisfy one's insatiable material desires. We'll see in a few days how living in this mode separates one from Krishna and binds one to this material world, resulting in repeated births and deaths.

The mode of darkness is the mode in which a person is unconcerned about the distinction between right and wrong. He becomes lazy and wants to enjoy life to its fullest. Yet, he does not want to put in any effort; and so he engages in unhealthy practices. His intellect is obscured by the dust of delusion to the point that he only thinks for himself and no one else.

People living in the mode of purity are difficult to find today. Who cares about pure spirituality and morality? Religion has turned into a means of gratifying one's material desires. Today, goodness and austerity are unusual qualities.

The majority of us exist either in a state of passion or in a state of darkness. The ones who live in the mode of passion work very hard (often *too* hard) to preserve their 'standard of living,' which is mostly concerned with keeping up with their wealthy neighbors. They may act as if they're 'enjoying' their lives, but they know deep down in their hearts that they are spending a large part of their lives in slavery.

However, those who live in the mode of passion are still better than those living in the mode of darkness. The latter live their lives as parasites, preying on others. They seek shortcuts by stealing, and even killing, for what is not rightly theirs to enjoy. They have no moral compass. They are a burden on this planet, and they undoubtedly pay heavily for their karmas in their current or future lifetimes.

It's worth noting, however, that no one in this material universe possesses only one of these attributes. All of us are a combination of the three modes, though in different proportions. We all have both positive and negative traits. However, it is *our* responsibility as humans to make sure the pure qualities triumph over the impure.

We've already seen how a person's mental tendencies at the time of death influence his spiritual growth. Krishna confirms this once more in the following verses:

"When an embodied one undergoes death while the mode of purity is predominant (in his mind), then he attains to the spotless worlds of the 'knowers of the highest' (like the learned sages). Undergoing death in the predominant mode of passion, one is born among those attached to action. Similarly, dying in the predominant mode of darkness, one is born in the womb of the unintelligent (like animals, etc.)." [BG 14.14-14.15]

But now comes the big revelation —

There is an even higher state of being than the three modes of material nature.

Krishna says, "When a seer sees no other performer than the modes of material nature, and knows Him (Supreme God) who is higher than these modes, he attains My nature. The embodied (the soul) having transcended these three modes of material nature, from which the body originates, is freed from birth, death, decay (old age), and sorrows (resulting from them), and experiences immortality." [BG 14.19-14.20]

This is the progress we should aim for. Rising beyond the three modes — even of purity — should be the goal. But what qualities does a person who has transcended the material modes of nature possesses that one should aim to develop? When Arjuna asks this to Krishna, Krishna replies with a long list of the qualities of such a realized soul (we will look at those qualities on Day 12). He says that such a person is unaffected by the constant flow of sense desires, being aware that such desires are caused by the modes and he need not be disturbed by them. As a result, he remains steady in all situations — whether these situations seem to be happy or sad. For such a person, there is no difference between gold and a pebble, praise and blame, honor and dishonor, friend and enemy. He is always engaged in loving service to God, and thus attains perfection.

Are you ready to be that person?

Key Takeaways

1. Purity, passion, and darkness are the three modes of material nature.

2. We are all made up of these three modes, albeit in different proportions.
3. We have a responsibility to ensure that the mode of purity dominates our minds.
4. Our true responsibility, however, is to rise above the three modes with the help of divine spiritual wisdom, recognizing the bounding nature of the three modes and dedicating ourselves to Krishna. This is the path that leads to spiritual perfection.

Day 11: Always Choose Right

"Arjuna asked: Those who, setting aside the regulations of the scriptures, perform sacrifice with faith — what is their state, O Krishna? Is it *sattva*, *rajas*, or *tamas*?" [BG 17.1]

The ability to differentiate between right and wrong, and always choosing what is right, is one of the fundamental qualities of a pure devotee. It's a sign that his intellect is top-notch and that his mind isn't tainted. It's a sign that he's come a long way in his search for Krishna, and chances are he'll make it to his true home.

In the Bhagavad Gita, Lord Krishna describes this quality in great detail for the sake of all mankind. He speaks about what is pure faith, pure food, pure spiritual practices and sacrifices, pure austerity, pure charity, and so on. Let us consider a few examples of what the Lord says in this regard.

Faith - "O descendant of Bharata, the faith of each is in accordance with his nature. This man (human being) is made up of faith; what his faith is, that verily is he. Those in the mode of purity worship the demigods; those in the mode of passion, worship nature-spirits and ogres; and the others, those in the mode of darkness, worship the spirits (of the dead) and a host of ghosts." [BG 17.3-17.4]

Food - "Foods that increase the duration of life, purity, strength, health, happiness, and affection, that are succulent, oleaginous, enduring, and agreeable, are dear to those in the mode of purity. Foods that are bitter, sour, salty, very hot, pungent, dry, and burning, are dear to those in the mode of passion, producing sorrow, grief, and disease. Foods that are not properly cooked, tasteless, putrid, and stale, and also remnants (of food eaten by others), and impure food, are dear to those in the mode of darkness." [BG 17.8-17.10]

Spiritual Practices and Sacrifices - "The sacrifice offered by those who are devoid of desire for rewards, performed in accordance with the scriptural regulations, with a mental conviction that it must be performed as it is surely a duty, is in the mode of purity. But that sacrifice which is performed seeking reward, as also for ostentation, O highest one in the dynasty of Bharata, know that sacrifice to be in the mode of passion. They (wise men) consider the sacrifice performed without scriptural regulations, without distribution of food (offered in sacrifice), without chanting of hymns (Vedic verses), without offerings (to the priests), and without faith (in God), to be in the mode of darkness." [BG 17.11-17.13]

Austerity and Penance - "Worship of the demigods, the twice-born (Brahmins), the spiritual masters, and the wise (those having knowledge of spiritual truths), purity, straightforwardness, celibacy, and non-injury (to the innocent beings), are said to be the "austerity of the body." Speech that is not agitating, and is truthful, pleasant, and beneficial, and the practice of the study of the scriptures, are said to be the "austerity of speech." Tranquility of the mind, gentleness, silence, self-control, purity of nature — these are said to be the "austerity of the mind." This threefold austerity practiced with transcendental faith by men devoid of desire for rewards, they (wise men) call being in the mode of purity. The austerity which is practiced for gaining good reception, honor, and worship, and verily, with ostentation, is here said to be in the mode of passion — and they are unstable and fleeting. That austerity which is practiced out of foolish intent of torture of oneself or destruction of others, that is said to be in the mode of darkness." [BG 17.14-17.19]

Charity - "The gift which is given knowing that it ought to be given (as a righteous duty), without an expectation of return, at a proper place and time (to make sure of its proper use), and to a worthy person — that gift is considered to be in the mode of purity. But that gift which is given with the aim of getting something in return, or again desiring some reward, and is given reluctantly, is considered to be in the mode of passion. That gift which is given at an improper place and time (which may be detrimental to its proper use), and to unworthy persons, or without respect, with disdain, is considered to be in the mode of darkness." [BG 17.20-17.22]

Further, in Chapter 18, Lord Krishna instructs us how we can separate knowledge, action, performer of action, intelligence, fortitude, and happiness into the three modes of material nature.

I understand that remembering all of this is difficult, and Krishna knows that as well. And it is for this reason that He has provided us with a compass that can always point us in the right direction, but only if we are willing to use it. That compass is our conscience. That is what we should consult when we are not sure about our conduct. That is what we should make our everyday companion when making decisions about our actions. And if we use this God-given powerful tool, we can never go wrong.

We can see exactly where Krishna wants to lead us. He wants us to stay in the zone of purity and goodness. He looks for noble values that are free from material adulteration. Purity in faith, food, austerity, spiritual practices, charity, knowledge, action, intelligence, fortitude, and happiness makes a devotee fit for the next stage of spiritual progress — to rise above the three modes of material nature.

A person seeking liberation must rise above these modes (even the mode of purity). Then he is said to have evolved from being material to being divine. But, before getting to that point, one must maintain a high level of purity by always choosing the pure over the impure, the positive over the negative, and the right over the wrong. This is a requirement that cannot be avoided. Only a pure-hearted soul can transcend these material modes and approach Krishna.

Key Takeaways

1. One must cultivate pure mental and physical qualities and always perform his duties in the mode of purity.
2. Choosing pure over impure is a necessary prerequisite for transcending the modes of material existence and progressing closer to Krishna.

Day 12: Divine vs Demonic

"The divine attributes are for liberation, the demonic attributes are considered to be for bondage. Do not grieve, O Pandava (Arjuna), for you are born with divine attributes." [BG 16.5]

The Bhagavad Gita is basically a how-to manual for living a perfect life. And to live a perfect life, we need to develop the *qualities* that make our lives perfect. But before developing those traits, we need to be *aware* of the traits that we should strive to develop, and the ones we should avoid.

Lord Krishna has made our task very simple by telling us exactly what divine qualities we need to have in order to live an ideal life in this material world, as well as the demonic characteristics we must escape at all costs.

So what exactly are those divine and demonic attributes? Let's see.

In the sixteenth chapter of the Bhagavad Gita, Lord Krishna enumerates the Godlike, spiritual, and transcendental attributes of a realized soul, which include:

1. Fearlessness
2. Purity of heart
3. Knowledge
4. Steadfastness in Yoga (of meditation)
5. Charity
6. Self-restraint
7. Religiousness
8. Interest in studying scriptures
9. Self-discipline
10. Straightforwardness
11. Noninjury to the innocent beings
12. Truthfulness
13. Absence of anger
14. Renunciation
15. Peacefulness
16. Absence of fault-finding and slander
17. Compassion toward all beings
18. Noncovetousness
19. Gentleness
20. Modesty
21. Steadiness
22. Vigor
23. Forgiveness
24. Fortitude
25. Purity (of body and mind)
26. Absence of hate
27. Humility

On the other hand, the demonic characteristics that one should not allow into one's mind include:

1. Egoism
2. Arrogance
3. Conceitedness
4. Anger
5. Harshness
6. Ignorance
7. Absence of knowledge of the difference between right and wrong
8. Impurity
9. Improper conduct
10. Lack of truth
11. Atheism
12. Lustfulness
13. Atrociousness
14. Destructive nature
15. Dishonesty
16. Selfishness
17. Overambition
18. Delusion
19. Stubbornness
20. Hypocrisy
21. Forcefulness
22. Lasciviousness
23. Cruelty

The great thing is we already know that the good qualities mentioned by Krishna are possessed by the virtuous, while the bad qualities are possessed by the devilish. However, we also know deep down that we will die, but we don't consider it as we go about our everyday lives. Knowing anything but not putting it to use is the same as not knowing it at all. And it is for this reason that the compassionate Lord Krishna reminds us to take this seriously.

I won't go into detail about these characteristics. These are fairly easy to understand. And God has already given us a shortcut that eliminates the need for us to memorize this list of good and bad qualities. And that shortcut is our conscience (as I mentioned yesterday), which we are all born with.

Krishna further tells us, "I hurl forever those cruel haters, the worst among men in the material world, the evil-doers, verily, into the demonic wombs (in their coming lives). Entering demonic wombs (being born in demonic species) birth after birth, the fools (the ignorant ones), not attaining Me, O Kaunteya (Arjuna), reach even lower conditions (species)." [BG 16.19-16.20]

This is clearly a situation nobody would want to be in. So now is the time to make the necessary character adjustments. We don't have time to waste.

In verse 16.21, Lord Krishna speaks of the three gates to hell, which every sane person must attempt to abandon immediately, as they lead to the degradation of the soul. These are —
  1. lust,
  2. anger, and

3. greed.

Avoiding these goes a long way in the successful progression of the soul to the highest destination — the home of the Lord.

So, the Lord has left nothing to our guesswork. He has clearly outlined what makes up appropriate and inappropriate conduct. If we still cannot make our lives spiritually successful, we would only have ourselves to blame. He has done His part. Now it's our turn.

Key Takeaways

1. Lord Krishna has clearly jotted down the divine and devilish qualities we should develop and avoid, respectively, for our reference. It is our job to make sure we abide by His instructions.
2. Those who disobey these guidelines descend into the lowest modes of existence, and their chances of attaining Supreme consciousness become slim.
3. Lust, anger, and greed are the three gates to hell. At all costs, we must prevent these from invading our minds.

Day 13: The Purpose of Life

"Those whose intelligence is immersed in That (the Supreme God), soul is one with That, faith is given to That, who have taken That as the supreme goal, their sins being cleansed through knowledge, reach the state of no return." [BG 5.17]

We're just like Arjuna in that we're worried about our own lives and the lives of our loved ones. And all of our big decisions are only by-products of this fear (even though it doesn't always look that way). We are all bewildered. It's a different matter that our egos don't allow us to accept this fact.

Most of us live our lives in utter randomness and chaos, with no particular goal in mind. Even if we have a goal, it is a materialistic and short-term one — building a house, earning a million dollars a month, raising a child to be a doctor, being the world's richest person, and so on. There is nothing wrong with such plans, except that they are insufficient on their own. These may be noble goals; but these need to have a supplemental goal — a goal that aligns with the goal which our manufacturer has set for us — a goal, achieving which our lives would be successful in the true sense.

Most people delude themselves into believing that there is no such thing as a higher purpose. This way they relieve themselves of the pressure of thinking differently about themselves, their lives, and their aspirations. Most of us set mundane objectives for our lives. Take birth (which we don't seem to control), play, go to school and college, get a degree, marry, work, gain wealth, enjoy, retire, and die. Sounds like a plan, doesn't it? But to what end does it lead? Nowhere. Can something be its own purpose? Obviously, no. So how can life be its own purpose? How can it be rational to live simply for the sake of living? Like anything else, the purpose of life has to be something outside of life — something bigger. Think about it.

If you believe there is a creator or God, then does it make sense to you that God sent you on this planet just to work and to have fun? What benefit will this have? What purpose will this serve? Absolutely nothing if you ask me. Imagine God telling you, "I am sending you to this planet called Earth. Go there, work hard, have lots of fun, and then come back. Then I will send again to that planet and it will be a never-ending cycle." You ask God, "But why do you plan to do that? What good will it do to keep sending me to the same place again and again?" And God replies, "Nothing. It will just be so much fun."

God does not send souls on this planet for His own amusement. He sends us because _we desire to come here_. God is merciful. When a soul desires to explore material life, God does not argue. He sends the soul to this world, gives it a body, and lets it experience the material planet. But God takes away one thing — the memory. We become forgetful of our true nature. And then we suffer, whether or not we acknowledge it. According to verse 8.15 of the Bhagavad Gita, this world is a "temporary place full of miseries." We, the souls, then crave liberation. And there is just one way to attain freedom from all this misery — remembering our true nature.

The purpose of our lives is to understand who we truly are, who God is, and what our relationship with Him is, and then to develop such a deep love for Him that we desire to break free from the cycle of birth and death and live with and serve Him forever.

In a way, it's a test of whether we'd choose God or pleasure if given the option. God offers us the choice of choosing Him over everything else. He attaches us to things while still giving us the freedom to break free. Then it's up to us to determine whether or not we want to be free. It's like buying an ice cream cone for your kid and then asking him if he wants to return it to you. If he wishes to do so, you are unquestionably more important to him than the ice cream. The love of the child for you is pure and unconditional, and so he is deserving of special attention and affection.

The next question you might have is: "If I pass the test, what reward does God have in store for me?" The answer is liberation from the never-ending cycle of life and death and the opportunity to serve Him forever.

Why did God create this world and living beings?

If you believe there is a God, do you also believe God can act without a greater reason in mind? It is self-evident that if there is any supreme force, it must have a vast amount of intelligence, several times greater than the collective intelligence of all living beings on this planet. Will such an intelligent person or power ever do something just at random, without an important purpose? I don't think so.

So, if every behavior of God must have a cause, what was the *reason* He created everything, including the universe, this world, and us? Let us investigate and discover the reason for creation.

Consider it. Is it possible to be a father without having a child? The child is the one who grants the father the title of 'father.' It is the child who bestows upon the father the duties of a father as well as the joys of becoming a parent. There can be no father if there is no child. Similarly, there would be no God if there were no beings subordinate to Him. Only if there is someone who can call God "God" can He be considered as God.

Now it's not that God created us to satisfy His ego. He created us to give *Himself* a purpose. Suppose there was no life at all. What would have been the basis for God's existence? Nothing. He exists for us and we exist for Him.

But then He could have made us and have us live with Himself. What was the need to create this material world? He created the material world to fulfill *our* wishes. It's us who wished to enjoy ourselves without God, believing that we could be content without Him. We desired to live our lives on our own terms. We wished to forget God and have fun in a different world. This world we live in is a product of such a wish of the soul. This material world is where God sends us when we desire to live away from Him, and it is only here that we can recognize our error and work to return to Godhead.

The Divine purpose

We are nothing but God's own pieces, containing a tiny fraction of His total energy. He is the totality of everything that has ever existed, is currently existing, and will ever exist. We are just a small part of the bigger picture. But if God is all conscious, He would want His 'parts' to be all conscious too. That is the reason He sends us on this planet — to test ourselves in the material world and then ultimately pass the test by regaining our consciousness and as a result, go back where we belong.

The Bhagavad Gita makes this very clear. It clearly says that this world is *duhkhalayam asasvatam* — a temporary place full of miseries. Lord Krishna says, "Having attained Me, the great souls, having reached the highest perfection, never take birth again in the temporary place full of miseries (the material world)." [BG 8.15]

This is one of the Bhagavad Gita's most significant verses. In some other verses, Krishna reiterates what He says in this verse. However, the way He puts it here makes our purpose clear to everyone who is conscious and prepared with an open mind.

In Sanskrit, the terms *sasvatam* and *asasvatam* mean 'permanent' and 'temporary,' respectively.

It should not be too difficult to understand why Krishna refers to this world as temporary. So far in my life, I've met many people. Many of them are no longer alive and the rest of them, including myself, will be dead soon.

You like it or not, after a hundred years from today most, if not all, of the people you know today, no matter how much you love them, would be dead. God places us in this world for a small period. You see, the test can't go on indefinitely. And He has created no device that allows us to transport anything from one world to the next. As a result, each of us should treat the planet as a temporary venue, similar to an examination center. We go to the examination center, complete our papers, and return home. We do not make it our home. However, because of memory loss, we believe this planet is our permanent home. We enter this world and quickly begin to associate ourselves with temporary objects. I am his son, and this is my country, my home, my degree, my designation, my name, and so on. We forget that even the bodies we live in are not ours; so how can all these be ours?

Duhkh means 'misery' and *alayam* means 'place.' Now, why does Krishna call this planet a "place full of miseries?" After all, Krishna created this world Himself. Why would He create something and then call it a place full of miseries? Why would Krishna create a world which is not perfect?

This is something most of us get wrong. This world is, without a doubt, a perfect place. This is the best location for Krishna to bring us to the test. This world was supposed to be flawed and full of sorrow. It is, in reality, very much so. This world is perfectly imperfect. Krishna made what He wanted to make.

Now many of us consider this world to be a wonderful place to live. It has mountains, trees, lakes, fishes, animals, greenery, nature, rain, clouds, rainbows, and rivers. Again, today we have television, Netflix, the internet, mobile games, PlayStation that helps us have a good time.

Yes, certain natural and man-made objects can temporarily relieve our pains. But how long do their effects last? Not for long. They are just temporary solutions to a permanent problem — and that problem is pain. No matter how much we deny it, all we do in our lives is trying to reduce the amount of pain we feel.

Most of us refuse to acknowledge that the world is full of suffering. The self-help industry is riddled with content that leads us to believe that the universe is brimming with happiness for those who pursue it. They instill in us the importance of being 'positive' at all times. "Look for the bright side," they advise. But isn't concentrating on the positive a way to distract ourselves from the pain that life (which, whether or not we like it, contains many negatives) causes?

Accepting this planet as a source of suffering is considered a pessimistic way of living. But avoiding the actual world and chasing after the unreal isn't optimism; it's suicide.

Accepting things as they are (rather than believing just what one *wants* to believe in — a rosy picture, and denying what is painful) and then searching for the best solution is a much more positive way to live one's life. This way, one can avoid the agony of self-misguidance.

We are born in our mothers' wombs, and our excruciating journeys start at that moment. We have little space there, so we have to make do with the leftovers of whatever our mothers eat. Urine, stool, and blood are everywhere around us. And the first thing we do when we emerge from that hellish place is let out a long scream. When our mothers hear our cries for the first time, they become delighted. But our cries are just an expression of pain, the result of a torturous experience we've been going through for months. That is how a human's journey on this planet starts.

Then our actual struggle begins. To live and prosper, we must learn a great deal. To provide for ourselves and our families, we must work hard. Meanwhile, we must take care of our bodies, and if we become ill, our suffering worsens. We have to struggle through life and then enter old age when life becomes even tougher. The body deteriorates, teeth fall out, joints become weak, we struggle to walk, sleep becomes difficult, and we become dependent on others. And finally, we see death staring at us, which again is painful.

Of course, we enjoy ourselves as well. However, whether we watch a movie, go on holiday, go to a pub, play football, or read a book, what we are essentially trying to do is diminish our pain, whether or not we realize it. These are like the pain relievers that a doctor would prescribe for a patient with chronic neck pain. It will temporarily relieve the patient's pain, but the patient is aware that the pain will return.

And there's one more thing that needs to be mentioned. Painkillers can provide temporary relief, but if used for an extended period, they become a habit — a dangerous habit. The patient becomes a slave to it. Without the painkiller, the patient has a hard time surviving. The same goes for these objects of sense gratification.

Surgery, however, is a safer option. At first, it may seem to be a daunting process to go through. However, it proves to be a lifesaver in the end.

Krishna says, "They who, through the eye of knowledge, know thus the difference between the 'field' (body) and the 'knower of the field' (Supreme Soul — God), and understand the process of attaining liberation from the 'nature of the being' (material nature), reach the Supreme." [BG 13.35]

Our goal is to achieve self-realization through awareness. Our goal is to keep our minds free of emotional attachments to things that aren't ours. Our goal is to learn more about Krishna and get to know him better. Our goal is to liberate ourselves from material slavery and the never-ending cycle of birth and death. Our goal is to be free of this planet and go back home.

Let me sum up our life's ultimate mission because it is far too important to be overlooked:

ATTAINING KRISHNA IS THE SOLE PURPOSE OF OUR LIVES.

Now I did not say that it is the most important purpose. I said it is the *sole* purpose. So what I am saying is that attaining Krishna is the *only* purpose of a human's life. I know that is a bold statement. What about incredible accomplishments such as finding planets and visiting them, inventing medicine to treat life-threatening illnesses, developing a country's economy, and winning Wimbledon?

These may be significant accomplishments for us as humans who live in a materialistic world; but not for God. Krishna calls attaining Him as achieving the highest perfection. And how can He expect anything less from us than achieving the highest perfection? If we are His creation, we should expect Him to hold high standards for us. Winning Wimbledon may seem significant to us, but to God, it is no different from any other human activity that satisfies his need for monetary benefits and ego gratification.

Even ostensibly worthy causes, such as developing life-saving drugs, are only worthwhile when they are accompanied by the desire to achieve the highest level of perfection. If God is the most perfect of all (which is very obvious) and we do not attain Him, then it is obvious that we cannot consider the purpose of our lives to be complete.

Here's what I write in *Bhagavad Gita - The Perfect Philosophy*:

Most of us set mundane goals for ourselves, such as making a lot of money, settling in a country or city that we love, buying a huge house, owning a dream car, marrying the boy or girl of our fantasies, retiring with a large bank balance, or even taking the last ride in a golden coffin!

Others have grander ambitions, such as discovering the cure for cancer, establishing a free hospital for the poor, winning an Olympic medal for their country, raising a child to become a doctor, and so on.

But all of these aims and ambitions, even the nobler ones, suffer from one basic flaw. Working for them is perfectly fine, but these are not enough to make one *spiritually* successful. In other words, those are not our *divine* goals.

How can they be? Can something be its own purpose? Of course, no. Will you be satisfied if you build a free hospital to help the needy, but no one shows up for treatment? The establishment of the hospital was not the real purpose you had in mind. The real purpose was to provide free treatment to the poor, which is something *external* to the establishment of the hospital.

Now, if nothing can be a purpose in and of itself, how can anything you start and finish in this life be the goal of your life? The goal of life must be something that exists outside of life, something that extends *beyond* life.

Most of us do not even consider the possibility of having a higher purpose, let alone the consequences of failing to achieve it.

Some of us believe that the purpose of life is to live morally and to help others. And some say that the goal is to keep our minds free of any negative thoughts.

While it is all good to be ethical, serve others, and keep one's mind pure through meditation and mindfulness, none of these extend beyond material life.

The Vedic teachings, including the Bhagavad Gita, also encourage us to live morally and to keep our minds free of negativity. In fact, the Bhagavad Gita provides clear instructions about what constitutes good charity and good meditation. These scriptures do not, however, consider any of these to be the ultimate goal of our lives. They consider these, at best, as means to an end. As I already stated, our purpose cannot be limited to material existence. It is something a lot bigger than that.

According to Srimad Bhagavatam, "The pursuit of pleasure should never be the goal of life. Because the aim of human life is to enquire about oneself and utter truth, one should only be concerned with maintaining one's health. Nothing else should serve as a source of motivation for one's behavior." [SB 1.2.10]

Isn't it self-evident? You sit for an exam to pass it. Is passing the test, however, a goal in and of itself? You want to pass the exam because you want to progress to the next level, or because you want to earn a degree that will help you get a good job. Again, you put a lot of effort into your business or job. Is working hard, however, a goal in and of itself? Obviously not. You put forth considerable effort to get a promotion that will allow you to earn more money or to improve the profitability of your company. Every activity has a purpose, but the purpose does not lie within that activity, but outside of it.

So, if that's the case, how can life have a meaning in and of itself? It should go without saying that the goal of life must be something larger, grander, and more meaningful than life itself. The goal of life must be to reach somewhere beyond one's own self and to accomplish something greater.

And you now know what it is.

Key Takeaways

1. No matter how grand the goals we've set for ourselves seem to be, those are not the goals for which we take birth in the material world. At best, they might be the means to an end.
2. No matter how wonderful this material existence may seem to us, and how much we try to ignore the pains, the fact remains that this world is a temporary place full of miseries.
3. Our true purpose is to gain transcendental knowledge, become free from the cycle of birth and death, attain Krishna, enter His divine abode, and live there as His servitor forever.

Day 14: True Knowledge

"When your intellect crosses the darkness of delusion, then you shall become indifferent to all that is yet to be heard and all that has already been heard." [BG 2.52]

You've figured out what you're here for. But what is the best way to achieve that goal? The Bhagavad Gita provides a detailed answer to this question.

The six principles of self-realization

In the Bhagavad Gita, Lord Krishna explains the process for breaking free from the cycle of birth and death, as well as the path to Him. After reading the Gita for many years, I believe there are six fundamental principles that a seeker must follow in order to attain liberation from this material world. I call this set of principles "the six principles of self-realization." These are:

1. Developing true knowledge

2. Freeing oneself from the results of one's work

3. Freeing oneself from sense gratification and attachment

4. Keeping oneself steady in all situations

5. Freeing oneself from negative emotions

6. Engaging oneself in devotional service to Krishna

After studying the Gita, hearing it from many saints, and studying over a hundred books on this subject, I am convinced that if one follows these six principles of self-realization, he will certainly attain Krishna and fulfill the purpose of his existence. Krishna mentions quite a few prerequisites for self-realization in the Gita. These six, however, are the most important and cover all else. As a result of developing these qualities, other qualities will develop as well. Then one can call himself a *Yogi* (one who strives for getting one with God).

For the next six days starting today, we will look at each of these six principles of self-realization, which can take us far in our spiritual quest.

We'll start with the first one today.

Developing true knowledge

If you've made it this far in the book, you shouldn't have any trouble grasping this concept.

We begin learning almost as soon as we are born, even if we are not aware of it. At home, we are taught to walk, talk, and follow directions. At school, we learn several languages, about various planets and the solar system, as well as the basics of physics, chemistry, and biology. We learn about incidents that happened thousands of years ago, as well as those that occurred in the last few hundred years. Then we go to college and choose our career paths and continue our education in our chosen field. Life also teaches us a lot. We learn from the successes and failures we see in our lives. We learn from how others treat us and how they treat each other. We learn from our own experiences and also from the experiences of others.

All this is great. But our true education only begins when we begin to enquire about our true self, the purpose of our lives, and the creator who watches over us all. Most people never do this in their lives, and so their education never even begins. I'm so glad you're taking the time to read this book. This is a sign that you possess the inquisitiveness necessary for achieving your life's purpose.

Lord Krishna says in the Bhagavad Gita, "O best among the descendants of Bharata, four kinds of virtuous men worship Me — the distressed, the seekers of knowledge, the seekers of wealth, and the wise. Of them, the wise, ever engaged in devotion, is the special one; for I am very dear to the wise, and he is dear to Me. All of these are indeed noble, but the wise I consider as My own Self; for being mentally steadfast, he is settled in Me as the highest goal." [BG 7.16-7.18]

What knowledge can be of greater value than the knowledge about the Absolute Truth? The knowledge we acquire at home, in school, or college is only useful when our hearts are still pounding. Once our hearts stop beating, all that knowledge becomes useless. Even if one does some monumental work in his lifetime which affects the lives of other beings even after he is gone, the lives of these beneficiaries would be incomplete without a knowledge of the self and the Supreme.

One must understand the difference between material knowledge and transcendental knowledge. The knowledge that Krishna talks about in the Gita is transcendental. This is the ultimate knowledge — the knowledge that helps one to do what he is here to do. One may be a brilliant scientist with material rocket science knowledge, but that knowledge would be of no benefit to him if it does not assist him in achieving his true goal.

Enquire about yourself. Enquire about God. Enquire about why you are here. Enquire about how you can achieve your purpose. This way, Krishna will direct you toward true intelligence.

Krishna says, "Even if you are the biggest sinner among all sinners, by the boat of knowledge, you will certainly be able to cross all oceans of sin." [BG 4.36]

This is the greatness of such knowledge that you may gain by the study of the Bhagavad Gita.

At the beginning of Chapter 7 of the Gita, Krishna says, "I shall declare to you in full this knowledge, combined with practical realization, which being known, nothing more remains to be known further here." [BG 7.2] And then, in the same chapter, Krishna declares, "After numerous births, the wise man attains Me, realizing Me to be everything. Such a great soul is very hard to find." [BG 7.19]

At the beginning of Chapter 9, Krishna again declares the knowledge He is about to impart as the most confidential one, understanding which one is relieved of the miseries of material life. He declares it to be "the sovereign education," "the sovereign secret," "the supreme purifier," and "eternal." Also, Krishna, in verse 9.17, declares Himself to be the object of all knowledge.

On Day 25, I will explain the importance of the knowledge shared by Krishna with Arjuna (and with us) in the Bhagavad Gita, and why it is the most ancient and perfect knowledge of all. For now, just make sure you understand what we discussed today, as this knowledge will enable you to grow and improve the other qualities needed for liberation.

Key Takeaways

1. Only when we begin to enquire about our inner selves, the purpose of our lives, and our Creator do we begin to receive meaningful education.
2. The Vedic scriptures contain the greatest of all knowledge, summarized by Lord Krishna in the Bhagavad Gita for the benefit of humankind.
3. Krishna is the object of all knowledge.

Day 15: Work. Not Results.

"Make happiness and sorrow, gain and loss, victory
and defeat the same; then, fight for the sake of
fighting. By so doing, you will not incur sin." [BG
2.38]

Krishna recommends one should act without consideration for the results of one's actions. This advice seems counter-intuitive to most seekers (and to all non-seekers). The fact is that this is one of the most misunderstood concepts given in the Bhagavad Gita.

Since childhood, we've been taught to act with the end in mind. A third of the self-help books in a bookstore claim to teach the best way to achieve one's goal. We study with the aim of passing the exam. We work for profits or promotion. We take a plane to get to our destination. Sex is a way for us to fulfill our senses. We watch a movie to pass the time. We read a book on spirituality to become more enlightened.

Whatever the activity is — small or significant — it must have a goal or outcome that serves as an incentive to carry it out. And then there's Krishna, oddly telling us to forget about the outcome and just keep performing our duties. How can this be logical?

Now please understand that Krishna never suggests ignoring the outcome. He suggests we stop *worrying* about the outcome. In other words, He advises we should act diligently, but that should be the extent of our concern. To pass the test, a student must prepare diligently. But his action is the only thing he should be concerned about. There should be no need to be worried once he has taken action and given it his all. He has no control over the outcome.

This may seem to be a piece of self-help advice coming from a popular motivational guru. But the reason Krishna advises us to develop this habit of giving up worrying about results is purely spiritual.

Concerning ourselves with the consequences of our actions ties us to this world. If you are worried about the consequences of your actions, it shows that you believe *you* are in control. Arjuna was concerned that if he fought the war, all of his loved ones would perish, including his grandsire, teachers, brothers, and other relatives. Krishna says, "Your right is indeed to perform dutiful actions, but not to the rewards. Never consider yourself as the creator of the rewards of actions, and there must never be an attachment to inaction." [BG 2.47]

Our ego always prevents us from thinking in this manner. We always assume (or are taught) that we have full control and power over our lives. We are often led to believe by self-help gurus that we have control over the effects of our actions. Yet we still know deep down that our *efforts* are under our control, but the *outcome* is decided by a force much greater than ourselves. We often see a worthy student being denied a distinction, a high-performing employee being passed over for a promotion, and the best player on the planet losing to a rookie. Right action does not guarantee immediate positive outcomes, but it does guarantee a positive move toward freedom, which is a much better outcome than anything we might hope for.

Instead of worrying about the result, work in devotion to Krishna. Dedicate the work and its result to Krishna. This is called Karma Yoga. This is one of the prescribed ways to reach Him. Work with a feeling that you are working to please God. This should serve as your motivation, and not the result. This is pure work. This is pure love.

But how to know what our proper duties are?

We now understand that we should act and devote our acts and their outcomes to Krishna without regard for the result. But how do we know which duty is the most appropriate for us?

According to Vedic literature, one should behave in accordance with his mental design. When society was run according to Vedic values, the society was divided into four groups: Brahmins, Kshatriyas, Vaishyas, and Shudras.

Brahmins were the religious leaders of the society. Kshatriyas ruled, managed, and protected the state from all kinds of threats. Vaishyas were farmers and traders. And Shudras engaged themselves in serving the other classes.

Lord Krishna advises in the Bhagavad Gita that one should act as per one's prescribed duties. He tells Arjuna, "Even, indeed, considering your specific duty (as a Kshatriya), you should not waver; for there is nothing better for a Kshatriya than a righteous war." [BG 2.31]

So, for knowing one's proper responsibilities, the Vedic scriptures advise us to consult our mental faculties, and once that is determined, one should work accordingly. One's God-given nature is the best source of knowledge about one's prescribed duties.

Krishna further says, "If, however, you decline to perform your duty to fight this righteous war, then having abandoned your duty and glory, you will incur sin." [BG 2.33]

Everyone has a set of responsibilities to which they must adhere, even though the outcome is entirely out of their control. You only have the right to carry out your responsibilities in order to achieve a goal. To get the best outcome, you must give your all and fight for it. However, you should be unaffected by the final outcome, whether it is favorable or not.

Krishna again clarifies, "Verily, no one can ever remain, even for a moment, without performing action; for everyone is compelled to act helplessly by the attributes born of (one has acquired from) material nature." [BG 3.5]

In other words, you should never ignore your prescribed duties and responsibilities.

And lastly, Krishna puts everything together and tells Arjuna, "Surrendering all kinds of activities unto Me, with your mind centered on the self (the soul), free from expectations (desires for favorable results), ego (sense of ownership), and feverish anxiety (worries about failure), fight." [BG 3.30]

Isn't this enlightening? Doesn't it set us free? Doesn't this make our lives so much easier? Doesn't it make our everyday decision-making quite effortless? All we now need to do is to reach out to our conscience and do as it says. All that is required of us is that we do the right thing. That is everything there is to it. Then Krishna may do as He pleases. And the good news is He is never wrong.

Key Takeaways

1. One should always strive to perform his prescribed duties.
2. However, one should devote these responsibilities and their outcomes to Krishna and not be concerned with the results of one's actions.

Day 16: Keep Senses in Check

"Whose endeavors are devoid of desires and purposes, and whose actions are burned in the fire of knowledge, he the sages call wise." [BG 4.19]

How do we experience anything in this world? It is, of course, through the sense organs of our bodies. We have a mouth to experience taste, a nose to experience odor, a pair of eyes to experience sight, skin to experience touch, and a pair of ears to experience sound. These organs are essential for us to function normally. Problems arise, however, when we become slaves to these organs.

It is the goal of our modern society to satiate these senses. We have a multitude of restaurants that serve a wide range of delicacies and have a nice ambiance in which we can thoroughly enjoy our meals. We have a wide variety of music to choose from to fulfill our need to hear something that matches our mood. We can have sex to satisfy our skin's desires.

However, the interesting thing to note is that we experience nothing outside of our minds. The taste we experience when we eat is actually experienced by our minds. Similarly, all the experiences of our ears, eyes, nose, and skin are actually experiences of our minds. These sense organs merely serve as a conduit for transmitting the information to the mind. We don't like our favorite food as much when we're in a foul mood. This is because our minds are cluttered, and we cannot completely enjoy the flavor. The food's flavor hasn't changed though.

Lord Krishna says, "O Partha (Arjuna), when one completely gives up all desires of the mind, and is satisfied in oneself through the realization of being a soul, then he is considered to be established in steady wisdom." [BG 2.55]

Now, why does Krishna say that we need to quit gratifying our senses to reach Him? Again, the answer is self-evident. If you are a person who enjoys mundane, earthly, material objects, you will remain bound to this planet. Why would you want to move to another planet if you are happy with this one? Perhaps the next world is much more majestic and beautiful, and this world is merely a shadow of it. But our senses keep us bound. They don't allow us to explore the truth. We don't want to believe there's something else out there.

Quitting sense gratification sets us free. It shows us how easy it is to live without succumbing to our senses. We can comfortably survive without foods that are too spicy, sweet, unhealthy, or non-vegetarian. However, considering their easy accessibility, it seems to be a waste of our taste buds if we do not enjoy them. We soon develop a deep desire for them.

We are constantly yearning for more and better. Nowadays, simple living is regarded as a negative way of living. The self-help industry thrives on the slogan, "always aim for more and better." But do we truly need 'more and better?' Is a dress that isn't a Gucci or an Armani isn't a dress? Is any meal that does not contain chicken or fish not worthy of being considered a meal?

Today we are always yearning for more and better things, and Krishna wants us to be free of this craving. We are only here for a short time, and we become enamored with these objects of sense pleasure as if nothing else exists. Money, power, a bigger home, a more expensive car, diamond jewelry, designer costumes, funky hairstyles, gold watches, expensive shoes, and an attractive spouse have all become common objects of desire.

We fill even our prayers with the desire for more and better. We don't want to attain God; we just want God to serve these things to us. How can we expect God to love us for this? Will you love your child if he just treats you as a supplier for his objects of desire? It is obvious that God loves one who is free from desire for material sense objects and loves Him in that state.

But giving up all desire is difficult. Suppose you decided yesterday that you will never eat non-vegetarian food again. On your way to work today, you could pass a well-known non-vegetarian restaurant. You find it difficult to ignore the aroma of chicken. You've been eating chicken for a long time. The scent appeals to you. It reminds you of the delicious flavor you used to love. But this is the test.

According to Buddha, all pain is caused by (material) desire. He was so right. I understand how difficult it is for you to envision a life without desires. But imagine that you have no desire left in your mind. Go to extremes. Imagine yourself not wanting anything — either for yourself or for anyone else. Remember that when you want anything for your loved ones, your family, your friends, your country, your community, or even the entire world, you are actually desiring it for yourself, as that will give *you* satisfaction. So free yourself from all of those desires as well, just for a few moments. Now, you want nothing for anyone. You are empty of any desire. You might become anxious. You had big dreams a few moments ago, and they were the driving force behind your hard work. You had goals and missions in mind. You had 'reasons to live.' Now you're left with nothing.

But hold on a second. Is it that important to have such desires? If you set your ego aside, you'll see that your desires have no bearing on your life. They are nothing more than objects of ego-satisfaction. We all suffer because we have made ourselves slaves of ego-satisfying objects. Even if you're trying to make someone else happy or give them a better life, you're ultimately feeding your own ego. Why does a person need so much that you must devote all of your time and energy to obtain it for him?

Marcus Aurelius says in *Meditations*, "The interval is so small between birth and death, and think with how much trouble and in company with what sort of people and in what feeble body this interval is laboriously passed. There is nothing to be excited about. For, consider the abyss of time behind thee, and the time before thee. In this infinity then what is the difference between living for three days or for three generations?" Remember, Marcus Aurelius was no ordinary man. He was the most powerful man in the world in his time. He had access to every object of pleasure present in those times. If he could understand the futility of sense gratification, why is it so difficult for us?

If it is you for whom you desire, it is you who needs to become conscious. If it is somebody else for whom you desire, both of you need to become conscious. If it is the world for which you desire, the entire world needs to become conscious.

Detachment from attachment

One significant form of sense gratification is attachment to others — my father, my mother, my wife/husband, my child, my siblings, my friends. It is relatively easier to free oneself from the desire for material objects, but freeing oneself from over-attachment to their dear ones looks to be a painful task for most spiritual seekers. It seems cruel to ask someone not to be attached to his family or friends. Why should one even attempt it? It seems to defy logic and reason. You might say:

"My parents have done so much for me, and now you are asking me to renounce them? Are you out of your mind?"

Or, "The so-called enlightened souls like the Buddha and Chaitanya Mahaprabhu were irresponsible crooks, who fled from their responsibilities for the so-called 'higher cause.' They left their young wives and small children to wander around in the woods. They needed to be punished for running away from their duties."

Before you jump to any conclusions, let me clarify that neither am I asking you to leave your parents, spouse, and child to 'wander in the woods,' nor am I demanding that you stop loving them. All I am asking you to do here is to carefully examine your feelings toward your loved ones in the light of your newly acquired consciousness.

When you recognize you are a pure spirit soul and that your body is merely a transient form that you have assumed in this world to work for your liberation, you must also accept that your loved ones are the same. They too are pure spirit beings who have come to this world temporarily. As a result, your physical relationship with them is also temporary. Yes, you are unquestionably linked. Your true relationship, however, is not what it seems to be on the surface. You're linked in the sense that you both come from the same source and have the same goal. The person who is mindful of this reality can truly be identified as conscious.

Love your dear ones. That is entirely fine. However, your affection should never take precedence over your awareness. You should be mindful that if your loved one is sad, it is actually his past karma at work. If he seems to be pleased, you should know it is not true happiness (unless he is living consciously), but again the temporary effects of his past karma. If he passes away, remember a soul has just left a body and will soon occupy another, either a physical one to return to the material world, or a spiritual one to return to Godhead.

I understand how tough it is. We've been conditioned to be attached to our family and friends since childhood. However, I warned you in the beginning that understanding the Bhagavad Gita's teachings would require a very open and accepting mind. But, if you want to live authentically and achieve your true purpose in life, you must learn to accept the facts, just like Arjuna. You must make use of this highest form of knowledge to make your life an example of enlightened living.

Key Takeaways

1. The desire for sense gratification is the biggest hurdle in our quest for liberation.
2. We need to be conscious of the true nature of everything and everyone we are attached to.
3. We need to quit gratifying our senses and replace that desire with a higher taste for spiritual awakening.

Day 17: Steady Mind. Wise Mind.

"One, by whom the world is not agitated, and who is not agitated by the world, who is free from the emotions of joy, sorrow, fear, and anxiety, is dear to Me." [BG 12.15]

All days of our lives are not the same. Sometimes we feel elated, sometimes we feel tired and out of spirits, sometimes we feel cheated, sometimes we feel happy. Whatever be the situation, if you know it does not mean much in the grand scheme of things, will it matter much to you?

Suppose you lose your job. You are worried about your future, and how you and your family will survive without income. But then you realize your situation is just a result of your past karma, and one just reaps what one sows, and that it is normal and it is how things happen and should happen, and that once your karmic effects are exhausted you will be free from misery. Will you still be worried as much? Will you panic if you know your situation is temporary, and this material situation will only take you closer to God, which is the true objective of your life? If you are aware of the laws of reality, you will not get worried for sure.

Now let us look at the flip side of the coin. Assume you've landed a profitable business deal that would almost certainly make you a lot richer. Are you not going to be ecstatic? You will, without a doubt. Will you still be elated if you know this achievement will have little direct impact on your spiritual progress, which is the only thing that really matters? If you are conscious, you would know that winning a large contract will increase your earnings, your business will prosper, and your future will be more secure, but all of this will simply serve as a means for you to survive so that you can achieve your ultimate goal. This is what will make you happy.

Let me quote a few verses from the Bhagavad Gita, where Krishna emphasizes the importance of stability in both happiness and sorrow.

"Verily, that man whom these (sensory perceptions) do not afflict, O best among men, the firm man who remains steady in sorrow and happiness — he is alone considered eligible for immortality (liberation)." [BG 2.15]

"One who is not shaken up by adversity, or hankers after pleasures in times of prosperity, is free from attachments, fear, and anger, is called a sage of steady mind. One who is free from attachment everywhere, neither joyous in obtaining anything good, nor hateful on meeting anything bad, his knowledge is considered established." [BG 2.56-2.57]

"Free from pride and delusion, having conquered the evil of attachment, absorbed constantly in the self (the awareness of being a soul), unattached to desires, free from dualities such as happiness and sorrow — the undeluded attain that imperishable state (of liberation)." [BG 15.5]

Reading these verses should make it clear why Krishna needs us to be steady in all circumstances in life, whether happy or stressful. True happiness can only come to those who want to grow spiritually and become more aware. What we normally call happiness is just pleasure, and pleasure and happiness are not the same. In fact, enlightened sages prefer the word 'bliss' to 'happiness.' There is a vast difference between pleasure and bliss. And we cannot be steady in mind if we do not understand this difference.

The first significant distinction between pleasure and bliss lies in their roots. The root of pleasure is commonplace and materialistic. The root of bliss, on the other hand, is what we understand as the root of everything — God. Getting a raise, landing a major deal, drinking and dancing in a pub, watching a movie, winning the lottery, are all examples of ways to feel pleasant. Is it sensible to equate finding joy in associating with God with the fun of dancing in a pub? Which is more pure and blissful? You know the answer.

The second big difference between the two lies in their longevity. Pleasure is fleeting, so it's important to switch up the source of pleasure regularly. Dancing in a pub can provide you with temporary pleasure for one or two nights. But will you get the same amount of enjoyment if you go there every night? Of course not. The law of diminishing marginal utility will come into effect. According to this law of economics, the utility gained from each subsequent use of something keeps decreasing. You'll begin to feel bored and yearn for a different source of pleasure. In reality, people who are overly reliant on such sources of pleasure often need breaks from them in order to rekindle their interest in them.

However, once you've tasted the ecstasy that comes from the ultimate source of all creation, you'll be free of the need for trivial pleasures. The permanent One then becomes the source of all your joy and happiness. He has always been and will continue to be there for you. He is the purest and the most beautiful being in the universe. And the bliss that emanates from Him is the purest and the most perfect of all feelings. Such bliss defies the law of diminishing marginal utility. It never gets boring and predictable. In reality, the more one knows about Krishna, the more one desires to learn about Him. That happiness is inexhaustible. That joy is infinite.

When one recognizes the mundane nature of worldly pleasures and begins to derive all of his happiness from Krishna, material pleasures lose their appeal. Promotion no longer excites him. He sees it as simply a product of his good work (karma), and he knows well that the results of this promotion, and the joy it brings, are temporary.

Similarly, worldly pain does not have any effect on a realized soul. Suppose he has a death in the family. Losing a loved one is painful. However, if a person knows that the body is transient, and the soul is eternal, and that the true purpose of life is to liberate oneself, pain loses its power. Such a person will pray for the soul's peace and avoid wasting time in grief.

It is only possible to be steady and maintain tranquility at all times when one is aware of the true nature of the soul.

Let's look at this from a fresh perspective. A conscious seeker knows well that he is a soul. This implies that he is neither his body nor his mind. Since he is not his mind, he is separate from his mind. Now happiness and distress are nothing but the opposite sides of the same coin. And that coin is the set of emotions existing in one's mind. Emotions live in the mind. Since he is separate from his mind, he is separate from his emotions as well.

However, it does not mean that a conscious person lives a mundane life, devoid of any emotions — just like a machine. In fact, it's just the opposite of the truth. A conscious person is always joyful, irrespective of his external circumstances. That is the effect of true spiritual knowledge. It liberates one from the turbulences of everyday emotions and places one in an eternal state of joy.

A conscious person understands that his pleasant and unpleasant feelings are just that — feelings. Emotions are simply a mental state. As a result of this awareness, a conscious person always remains in a state that is separate from his mind. Emotions of any kind, whether positive or negative, do not disturb his tranquility. By living in such a state, he remains protected from all suffering.

Key Takeaways

1. Only a person who is not disturbed by the constant flow of emotions and remains steady in all situations is fit for liberation.
2. To maintain the tranquility of mind, we must develop our knowledge of the self and the Supreme and the relationship between the two.

Day 18: Say "Bye" to Negative Emotions

"Being freed from attachment, fear, and anger, being fully absorbed in Me, taking complete shelter in Me, and sanctified by the penance of gaining knowledge, many have attained My nature." [BG 4.10]

The most brutal negative emotions are overindulging in sense gratification and being overly attached to material possessions. These are the most significant roadblocks to achieving spiritual wisdom. And we've already gone over how to deal with them in detail. However, this does not ensure your success. There are a variety of other emotions that can be just as damaging to your prospects of achieving your goal. According to Lord Krishna's instructions in the Bhagavad Gita, the main negative emotions from which one should stay away from are —

1. Fear,
2. Anger,
3. Envy,
4. Ego,
5. Greed, and
6. Excessiveness.

This point takes its roots from what we learned yesterday — keeping oneself steady in all situations. How can someone who is experiencing any of these negative emotions be steady?

The Bhagavad Gita advises a seeker to be mindful of the ill effects of these emotions. These emotions are nothing but mental impurities. It is impossible for a seeker to continue on the spiritual path in such a mental state. If one is unaware of the source and the nature of these emotions, they can be very difficult to deal with. Thousands of books have been written to help people deal with these emotions. However, in today's fast-paced world, these emotions can easily infiltrate one's mind, and, like termites, they can wreak havoc on whatever wonderful memories and thoughts one has carefully arranged there.

Even if one is not seeking spiritual advancement, protecting one's mind from such termite-like emotions is essential. These feelings are poisonous to one's happiness. Fearful people will never be confident in their work and relationships, and they will never advance in life. A person who becomes enraged over insignificant matters will never have good relationships with others. Envious and greedy people will never appreciate what they already have, and thus will never be satisfied. An egoistic person will always compare himself to others, which is a sure-shot recipe for failure. And someone who overeats and oversleeps will never be mentally or physically healthy. All of this leads to one thing — *unhappiness*.

I agree that it might not be possible to eliminate these feelings. But that doesn't mean they can't be treated and their ill effects can't be reduced to the point where they lose their ability to impair one's mental or physical health. This necessitates a thorough examination of these feelings, beginning with how they arise, how they corrupt one's mind, and how to protect oneself from their attacks.

The Source — There is one common source from which all negative emotions originate. The good news is that being aware of this one source can help us get rid of all of these negative emotions. And that source is *unconsciousness*.

Suppose a person is fearful of getting up in the morning because he does not want to go to the job he hates. Is it, however, the *job* that is causing the anxiety? While it appears to be so, it is not. The job is external to the person. Fear, however, is an emotion; which means the fear is internal. Anything external cannot influence the internal emotional state of a person unless he allows it to. Nobody willingly allows the external to affect his internal self. But we still make that allowance because of our nonconscious nature. If we are well aware of the facts ...

- that we are not our bodies,
- that this world is a temporary playing ground for us to make the best use of by achieving freedom from the continuous cycle of birth and death,
- that Krishna is the absolute truth, and we are His servants,
- that although it is not always evident, Krishna is looking after us all the time,
- that our suffering is just a result of our past karma,
- that the only thing that really matters is our consciousness of reality and there is absolutely no need to stress about anything else,
- that, if we love Krishna, we actually work for Him,
- that the actual source of our happiness is Krishna,

... how much fear, do you think, will then be left in our minds?

Fear (or any negative emotion for that matter) is just a result of one's emotional imbalance, which we call unconsciousness. A person with full knowledge of the Absolute Truth does not experience these emotions (at least not at the level others have to bear with them). In our example, if the person is conscious and feels uncomfortable in the morning while thinking about going to his workplace, he will tell himself —

- I am not this body. I am not what it seems to the outside world. I am a pure soul, and so are my bosses and colleagues.
- This job is simply a means of enabling me to preserve this body in order to free me from the relentless misery of life and find a permanent home at the feet of my Lord in His Holy abode.
- This world is anyway not my permanent home.
- I need to dedicate my work to Krishna, as per His instructions in the Bhagavad Gita.
- No matter what happens in the day, being a conscious being, I cannot really be harmed.
- This job is not important in the grand scheme of things.

In terms of source, consequence, and resolution, anger is very similar to fear. When a conscious person feels he has been harmed by another person, he would tell himself that the person who has harmed him is a pure soul like himself. He would sympathize with the person's unconscious existence and hope that he will be freed soon. If he is confronted with a situation where he feels unfortunate and therefore angry, he would convince himself that every kind of suffering is God's way of negating one's previous bad karma, and therefore is important for spiritual progress. As a result, there is no need to be upset because no harm has been done to him. He'll realize that any material damage he experiences will have no effect on his spiritual self, which is all that matters. So, there is no need to become enraged.

Let me present you with another viewpoint on this. A conscious person is devoid of desire (for himself and for others). Now, it is obvious that since he does not have any desire, he cannot have any enemies. Anyone can take anything from him, and because he is free of the desire for that thing, he will have no negative feelings toward that person. The result will be freedom from anger.

This does not, however, preclude one from fighting for his rights. It's only that he won't be disturbed on an emotional level, and his fight will be restricted on a physical level. In fact, a true yogi would pray, like Jesus, for the one who harms him, asking Krishna to provide the latter with knowledge of the self.

Ego, of all the emotions on the list, is the one that I believe does the most damage to one's spiritual growth. In fact, if one is free of ego, he can be free of all the other emotions on the list as well. This is because a big reason why emotions like fear and anger arise is that we identify ourselves with the body. This is nothing but ego. We recognize ourselves as a set of bones, skin, and blood. But this is not us. This is our body. Ego is the mistaken identification of oneself with one's physical body. If one is conscious, he will know that he is a spirit rather than a body. As a result, he will understand that nothing can really hurt his true self. If nothing can hurt his true self, fear and anger should obviously have no place in his mind. In this way, freeing oneself from the ego makes becoming free of the other negative emotions much easier and quicker.

One cannot be greedy once he is ego-free. That is because once one understands he is not his body, all objects of desire become meaningless. And when one's interest in sense objects disappears, greed can't possibly touch him.

Envy is also a product of one's ego and one's attraction toward things of sensual pleasure. Envy is a failure of a seeker in his spiritual progress. Envy is proof that the person is attracted to things meant for sense gratification — a bigger house, a more beautiful wife, a costlier car, a higher position in the company, and so on. That is his first failure. Envy also shows that the individual believes he is his own body. That's because if he knew that he is a soul, anything the other person possessed would have been meaningless to him. That is his second failure.

Excessiveness may not be an emotion in and of itself, but rather the product of one or more negative emotions. Krishna says, "But, O Arjuna, Yoga (of meditation) is not for one who eats too much, nor for one who does not eat at all, also not for one who sleeps too much, nor also for one who always keeps awake. For one who is moderate in his habits of eating and recreation, moderate in efforts in work, and moderate in sleep and wakefulness, Yoga (of meditation) becomes the destroyer of pain." [BG 6.16-6.17]

Indulging in excesses suggests a mental imbalance. And a mentally unbalanced person cannot hope to become a yogi. A yogi is someone who has total mental control and whose acts are always controlled and disciplined. He goes to bed and wakes up at the same time every day, eats well-balanced meals, and works just to keep his body going. Someone who sleeps too much is obviously unappreciative of the time he has been given. He has little concern for his own life. One who eats more than is needed is a slave of his tongue and stomach. He is more concerned with pleasing his senses, demonstrating that he is unaware of himself and his Lord.

Indulging in excessive recreation is common today. In fact, for most people, it has become their life's ambition. The aim of recreation is to keep one's mind fresh so that one can absorb the knowledge that will lead to his liberation.

However, there must be a limit on how much recreation one may engage in. That, however, is extremely rare. For example, once one starts playing video games to 'recreate' himself, it is common that he stops playing only after half the day is gone. That is not recreation; it is a waste of one of man's most precious resources — time.

Krishna warns against overworking as well. The objective of work is sustenance, but work has itself become the aim of living for most people these days. Sixteen-hour workdays are not uncommon now. When will one find time for self-discovery when one spends all his waking hours working? All motivational gurus encourage people to work hard. "Give it your all," they say. "Think big" is their mantra. All this is fine. My only question is if one spends all his time working, earns big, and then dies, without realizing who he really was, will his life be called a success? Think about it.

The Effect — If your mind is clouded by the dark smoke of rage, fear, envy, vanity, or excessiveness, you won't be able to see your true self. And the fact that we are ignorant of ourselves and our creator is the sole root of all the evil in the universe. This is a vicious cycle of cause and effect. Negative feelings hinder the acquisition of true knowledge and consciousness. As a consequence, there is more negativity — more hatred, fear, greed, and envy. People assume that others are their opponents, which leads to wars. That's an extreme form of anger. People are too busy deceiving others for their own gain to care about having an ethical mindset. What's the reason for this? People believe that having a lot of money and power is the most important thing. People are afraid of the future because, even though they worship an idol, they do not really believe in the presence of God. Many people worship because they make a calculation in their heads: "What if there is a God somewhere? Why take a chance? Let me pray to Him. If He's present, He could just give me what I want. If He isn't there I have nothing to lose." Real faith is hard to find. Real devotion is hardly anywhere to be seen.

The Solution — Do I still need to tell you the solution to all of this suffering? You should have guessed it by now. Yes, it is consciousness, enlightenment, awareness, eye-opening, realization, and cognizance. Call it what you want, its essence remains the same. This is the real solution to all problems. And why do I say so? Because when one achieves consciousness, one realizes that *there are no problems*. It is all in our minds.

A cancer patient may argue that all this consciousness stuff is nonsense. He may say, "Can't you see? All my hair is gone. I am extremely weak. I often have difficulty breathing and suffer from fever. And you say that this isn't a problem. Are you out of your mind?" If this is said to me, my answer would be, "Yes. I am out of my mind. Really. Because one has to step 'out of his mind' to know himself. Mind is where emotions live. And emotions, though necessary for survival on this planet, prevent one's eyes from seeing the truth. Be free from your mind and your emotions, and then you will really 'see.' Your present situation — be it good or bad in your opinion — is nothing but a result of your past karma (actions). What is there to feel bad about in that? Once you realize this, your only response should be happiness; because your past negative deeds are being negated, and you are becoming pure — all because of your current suffering. Use your suffering to become a better devotee. Use it to become more conscious. It will seem to be a problem only till the point you don't see properly."

This way of thinking is the key to overcoming your negative emotions. Turn the anxiety into knowledge. Convert your anger into awareness. Turn your ego into wisdom. Transform your greed into understanding. Convert your enmity into insight. Turn every negative aspect of your life into consciousness. Strive for enlightenment. Be fully aware of reality. Fill your entire self with knowledge. And once you discover yourself, hold on to that realization forever. This is the only solution.

Consciousness is the most powerful thing; because it allows you to see everything *as it is*. And, in reality, everything is good. Once you realize that, once you see that for yourself, and believe that without an iota of doubt, once you know and feel what being conscious is like, you become free. Consciousness liberates you from the limitations of external conditions. Once you start seeing things *as they are*, you will know that everything is great, and so you become free from negative emotions. When everything is good, what is there to be fearful of or be angry about? If you have all you need in abundance, what is there to be greedy about or be envious of? If you know that this body is not yours and that nothing in this world belongs to you or to anybody else, where lies the place for ego in your mind? Being free from all negative emotions that result in self-created suffering is blissful. And I want *you* to experience that bliss.

Key Takeaways

1. Negative emotions are significant impediments on the road to Krishna.
2. The source of all negative emotions is essentially the same — our unconscious nature.
3. Negative emotions destroy both our material as well as spiritual lives.

4. To get rid of these negative emotions, we must develop our spiritual awareness and live a conscious   life

Day 19: The Magic of Devotion

"By devotion, he (the perfected one) knows Me in essence — what and who I am. Then, knowing Me in essence, he enters into Me immediately after that."
[BG 18.55]

Today we will look at the last of the six principles of self-realization — engaging oneself in devotional service to Krishna.

Krishna loves devotion. He made this very clear when He sang the following verse:

"The Transcendental Person (God), O Partha (Arjuna), can be attained by unalloyed devotion to Him alone, within whom all beings dwell, and by whom all that exists (beings and objects) is pervaded." [BG 8.22]

Again He said, "Fixing your mind on Me, become My devotee; surrender to Me, and bow down to Me. Absorbing your self thus, and accepting Me as the supreme goal, you will surely come to Me." [BG 9.34]

Throughout Vedic literature, we find several instances where Lord Krishna speaks about His relationship with His devotees. When one is convinced that Krishna is God, the obvious next logical step is to submit to Him and devote one's life to Him. When one is certain that the purpose of his life is to return to where he came from, to return to Godhead, the logical next step is to do everything possible to achieve that goal. And a person cannot be considered conscious if he knows everything but does nothing about it. He can only be described as being in a semi-conscious state because he cannot think clearly.

However, there is one really important point I'd like you to keep in mind. The object of devotional practices should never be to receive something from God, *including liberation* from the material world. Devotion should be taken up out of love for Krishna. Love should be the only reason for devotion. Obtaining salvation should be considered as just an outcome of devotion — just a prize which a devotee may or may not be awarded. But that should not have any bearing on the quality of one's devotion. In fact, a true devotee will ask God for the full exhaustion of his punishment for his past negative karma. A true devotee strives for purity, which can only be achieved when the effects of all his past actions have been negated. And then his next desire is to serve Krishna forever, no matter how much pain he has to go through for this. A true devotee never asks to be relieved of the pain he deserves. His only ask is that Krishna helps him become a perfect devotee and accepts his love.

There are many ways you may develop devotion for Krishna. You should read Srimad Bhagavatam — the collection of all the pastimes of Lord Krishna. Reading Bhagavatam will develop your knowledge about the powers of Krishna and how blissful He is. You may attend Srimad Bhagavatam classes as well if you prefer hearing to reading. You should offer food to Him before eating yourself. You should decorate your house with His pictures and paintings. Fill your entire self with love for Krishna. See Krishna everywhere. And once you reach a stage where you are able to see Krishna in everything, then you will earn the right to call yourself a true devotee.

One simple method to develop a love for Krishna is to chant His name as a mantra on a daily basis. There are several mantras you can choose from. You can meditate on the first line of Srimad Bhagavatam, "*om namo bhagavate vasudevaya*" which means, "O my Lord, son of Vasudeva, I offer my respectful obeisances unto You." Or you can chant the mantra given by Lord Sri Chaitanya Mahaprabhu, the devotee-form of Lord Krishna — "Hare Krishna, Hare Krishna, Krishna, Hare. Hare Rama, Hare Rama, Rama Rama, Hare Hare." Or you may simply meditate on the syllable "Om." More important than the mantra is what goes on in your mind during the chanting of the mantra. You should ideally picture Krishna in His all-blissful form standing right in front of you, smiling. The aim is to fall in love with Krishna. And chanting His names and meditating upon His forms are the best ways to do this.

What to say when one talks to God?

Although we may pray in front of a statue daily, inside we do not really believe that a God exists. What I am saying may offend you, but it is a hard fact. If you truly believe in the existence of a power beyond comprehension, you will not treat it as merely a supply source for your needs. Listen to your prayers and you'll find that all you're asking for are temporary material things like good grades, a lovely wife, a rewarding career, an increase in pay, a stable future, and so on. Do you ever pray for the privilege of being able to serve God at all times? Is there anything in this world comparable to the ability to love God? Yes, I am not talking about God loving you. That's what everybody prays for, no matter how they may frame their prayers. I am talking about *you* loving God ... unconditionally. Now that's what a prayer should be.

God must know what you truly value, and He uses your prayers to find that out. So if you have the ability to serve God at the top of your list of desires, God will obviously love you. Actually, if you are perfectly conscious, you will not have a priority list at all. Because a list having just one item isn't a list. And the ability to serve God is the only desire of a fully conscious person. That is all he prays for, not for anything material, not even anything spiritual (like a place in God's abode), but just this — to be able to love and serve God till eternity. That's what you can call a perfectly pure prayer, free of all contamination of desires. This is the purest form of devotion.

Key Takeaways

1. Krishna loves pure devotion and His pure devotees.
2. You should cultivate an unwavering devotion to Krishna.
3. Your only wish should be to be able to serve Krishna forever.

Day 20: How to See God?

"Understand that just as the mighty wind, moving everywhere, rests always in the sky, similarly all created beings are situated in Me." [BG 9.6]

So you want to see God? You'll be happy to know that you're seeing Krishna at every moment, this present moment included. You're just not aware of it. The Lord says in the Bhagavad Gita, "O Kaunteya (Arjuna), I am the taste of water; I am the light of the moon and the sun; I am the syllable "Om" in all the Vedas; the sound in space; and virility in men. I am the sweet fragrance in the earth; and I am the luminescence in the fire; the life in all beings; and the penance in the ascetics." [BG 7.8-7.9]

Who doesn't drink water, see the sun's or the moon's light, or feel the heat of a fire? In reality, the very life inside us is a manifestation of Krishna. So how can we say we cannot see Krishna?

Yes, you may have a desire to see Krishna in His bodily form. However, that will need some effort on your part. Krishna has already clarified, "I am not manifest to all, veiled by My material (human-like) form. The deluded world knows Me not — the Unborn, the Imperishable." [BG 7.25]

What Krishna wants of us is to rid ourselves of our delusions and step into the light of knowledge and love for Him. Without proper light, we cannot even see our own hand, what to say of God. It's not even easy to see the powerful, famous, and opulent people in the world without powerful social connections, what to say of Krishna, who is the most powerful, most famous, and most opulent person in the entire creation. Krishna wants to have a personal relationship with everyone, but very few are even interested to know about Him. We don't seek Him out, so why should we be able to see Him easily?

There's a lot we can't see. We can't see the mind, emotions, thoughts, ambitions, or intelligence. We can only see their symptoms. The same is the case with the soul within the body, without which the insignificant material body has no value. We can feel the symptom of the soul — our consciousness. And we're surrounded by symptoms of the existence of God — innumerable life forms, elements, forces of nature, and space. Then, should we be able to see the source of all spirit and matter, the Supreme Soul, very easily? Even Arjuna needed special eyes provided by Krishna to see His Universal Form.

Krishna is easy to love when one makes himself conscious of who he and Krishna are. *Krishna* means 'all-attractive.' And because Krishna is all-attractive, all one has to do to be drawn to Him is open one's eyes, clear the smoke of material pollution, and he will see Krishna in His all-attractive form standing right in front of him, playing transcendental music on His flute.

The simple reason we can't see Krishna is that we haven't yet developed *sufficient interest* in seeing Him, and thus are not making the required effort with a loving heart. Even great sages who try to meditate on Krishna's form within their hearts for many years can't attain that divine vision without developing pure love for Him. Ultimately, if we want to see Krishna, it's up to us to behave in such a way that He will want to see us and give us the ability to see Him.

This is the only way.

Tomorrow, we'll delve deeper into this topic by looking at the various ways to reach Krishna, as described by the Lord Himself in His divine song.

Key Takeaways

1. Krishna, in His unmanifested form, is everywhere, and we see Him everywhere, even if most of us aren't aware of it.
2. Pure love for Krishna is what is needed to see Him in His bodily form.

Day 21: The Best Path to God

"O descendant of Bharata, take refuge in Him (the Supreme God) alone with your whole being. By His grace, you will attain the supreme peace, and the eternal abode." [BG 18.62]

Lord Krishna clearly explains all the ways to reach Him in the Bhagavad Gita. We've already taken a look at these methods. But, today, we'll compare these paths to see how realistic they are in today's times (Kaliyuga) and try to find the simplest and most rational path to God for you.

So, what are the various routes to Krishna? The four principal ways to reach Him, as stated by the Lord in Chapter 12 of the Bhagavad Gita, are:

1. Jnana Yoga (the path of knowledge)
2. Raja Yoga (the path of meditation)
3. Karma Yoga (the path of action)
4. Bhakti Yoga (the path of devotion)

Jnana (pronounced *gyaana*) Yoga is the practice of self-education about spiritual truths and the Lord. Raja Yoga refers to the practice of continuous meditation on the Lord. Karma Yoga entails engaging in ethical practice without expecting a positive outcome and dedicating all the work and its outcomes to Krishna. Bhakti Yoga is defined as the practice of loving devotion to Krishna.

For a seeker, these four ways are not mutually exclusive. In fact, a better way to understand them is to think of them as different *stages* in the progression of the spiritual intelligence of a seeker.

In the Bhagavad Gita, Lord Krishna describes these four stages of spiritual growth in the following verses:

"Fix your mind on Me alone, place your intelligence in Me; thereafter, there is no doubt that you will always dwell in Me alone (by attaining liberation). If, however, you are not able to fix your mind upon Me steadily, O Dhananjaya (Arjuna), seek to attain Me by the Yoga of practice (of bringing the focus back to Krishna). If you are unable even to practice, be intent on working for Me (by dedicating all actions to Krishna); for by even working for My sake, you will attain perfection. If you are unable to do even this, then taking shelter in Me, renounce the results of all work, being self-controlled (not hankering for the rewards). Knowledge (Jnana Yoga) is indeed superior to practice (of mind-control); meditation (Raja Yoga or Dhyana Yoga) is superior to knowledge; renunciation of rewards of actions (Karma Yoga) is superior to meditation; peace immediately follows renunciation." [BG 12.8-12.12]

"A Yogi (one who constantly meditates on the Lord) is superior to the ascetic (who does not pursue the Lord), is also superior to the men of theoretical knowledge, and is also superior to the men of action (motivated by rewards). Therefore, be a Yogi, O Arjuna. And of all types of Yogis, the one who, being full of faith, merging himself in Me, worships Me — he I regard as the most devout." [BG 6.46–6.47]

If these verses are read and understood, we find the following hierarchy of the levels of progress of a spiritual seeker:

Jnana Yoga > Raja Yoga > Karma Yoga > Bhakti Yoga

First, there's Jnana Yoga. A seeker develops a strong desire to learn more about himself and God. When he attains divine wisdom, he begins to meditate on the Lord, which is known as Raja Yoga. The need for pleasure and attachment, however, persists. As he advances in wisdom, he works for a living, but he purifies his deeds by dedicating them to the Lord and not caring about the results of his actions — a practice known as Karma Yoga. He continues to learn about Krishna and his pastimes while working and meditating on them. And when his intellect hits the tipping point of devotion to the Lord, he engages in

Bhakti Yoga, or complete devotion to the Lord, giving up all other desires and attachments. These are the stages of the growth of a Vedic spiritual seeker.

It is impossible for a mortal being to advance further without jnana, or knowledge of the truths about oneself, the Lord, their relationship, and the meaning of one's existence. Only by reading the Vedic scriptures and thus developing one's intellect would one be able to understand the significance of dedicating one's work to Krishna. And over time, while meditating on Krishna and working for Him, he gains more awareness and eventually falls in love with Krishna, to the point where he devotes his life to His service.

This is one of the most difficult topics in this divine song to address. Most seekers are perplexed as to which direction they should take to reach Krishna. However, you should now be able to grasp this without difficulty. Cultivate awareness about yourself and the Supreme, meditate on Him on a daily basis, work for Him while renouncing the fruits of your actions, and eventually, devote yourself to Him. This is the perfect way.

However, Bhakti, or devotion to Krishna, is the goal that you should strive for. To attain the desired level of devotion to the Supreme Lord, knowledge, meditation, and renounced behavior are just the progressive steps. Bhakti yoga, according to Ramanuja, a 12th-century philosopher, is the *direct* road to *moksha* (liberation from the cycle of birth and death). He claims, however, that only those whose intellect has been educated through experience, meditation, and action can perfectly practice Bhakti Yoga.

It is also difficult to achieve liberation in today's world by relying solely on knowledge, meditation, or action. We don't have enough time to educate ourselves with full Vedic knowledge, which comprises countless scriptures and verses that we cannot read and comprehend within one lifetime. Just meditating will not suffice, as our meditation will never achieve the desired perfection if we do not love God. Today, it is almost impossible for someone to produce work that is free of impurities. One has no choice but to actively or passively tell lies to customers, employees, employers, and clients. One has to manipulate others for profit. How can the Lord accept such work?

But it is very much possible for everyone to be purely devoted to Krishna. It doesn't take much. It's enough to chant His name, remember Him, and praise Him for a few minutes, with a pure mind. This is the path to freedom for us from this impure world. For us, devotion is the only way out.

Key Takeaways

1. There are four ways to attain Krishna — Jnana Yoga (Knowledge), Raja Yoga (Meditation), Karma Yoga (Action), and Bhakti Yoga (Devotion).
2. It's better to think of these as stages on the path to material perfection rather than mutually exclusive ways to spiritual freedom.
3. Bhakti, however, is the surest and easiest path to Krishna in Kaliyuga. The other three are there to assist a seeker in developing Bhakti for the Lord.

Day 22: Renunciation

"Arjuna said: O mighty-armed, O Hrishikesha (Krishna), O slayer of the demon Keshi, I wish to know distinctly the essence of *sannyasa* (the renounced order of life) and *tyaga* (renunciation)." [BG 18.1]

A largely misunderstood and misinterpreted concept in the Bhagavad Gita and the other Vedic texts is the concept of renunciation. Those who want to avoid doing their duty, use Vedic verses about renunciation to argue that Vedic philosophy encourages abandoning all work and running away into the woods.

So it becomes important to analyze this term in the proper context and with an open mind. This is a delicate idea that, if misunderstood, can result in complete destruction of one's material and spiritual future.

Lord Krishna beautifully describes this difficult-to-understand subject in Chapters 5 and 18 of the Bhagavad Gita.

Lord Krishna says, "But renunciation is hard to attain, O mighty-armed Arjuna, without Yoga (of action). By the practice of Yoga (of action), a sage quickly attains the Supreme. Engaged in Yoga (of action), a pure soul, being self-controlled, having control over his senses, and seeing his own self as the self of all beings (being aware that all beings are pure spirit souls), though performing actions, is never tainted (by the effects of Karma)." [BG 5.6-5.7]

Discussing the teachings given in Chapter 5, I write in my English translation of the Bhagavad Gita:

Also, what is important for us to realize is that we must give up a few things as soon as possible: a desire for objects that provide temporary and impure material pleasure to the senses, a desire for the rewards of actions, thinking of ourselves as bodies (and thus nurturing false ego and considering ourselves as the controller), and succumbing to negative mental attributes like anger. This, not the abdication of responsibility, is true renunciation.

Sannyasa (the renounced way of life) is described by Lord Krishna as "giving up all activities done *with the desire for results.*" Tyaga (renunciation) is described by Him as "giving up the desire for fruits of one's activities."

Krishna nowhere says that one should give up everything and live in a cave and meditate. In fact, He identifies three types of practices that should never be abandoned and should be carried out with purity and without regard for the outcome. These are:

1. Religious sacrifices,
2. Charity, and
3. Penance.

Renunciation involves a mental shift. We have already looked at the idea of renunciation in detail as part of the discussion on the second principle of self-realization. But today we need to understand that giving up the desire for results is not the same as giving up any righteous action. Lord Krishna did not order Arjuna to give up fighting and go to the forest to meditate. On the contrary, He urged him to carry out his responsibilities by fighting for the right cause.

So the concepts of tyaga and sannyasa do not advocate abdicating one's responsibilities. There are no excuses to run away from responsibilities, and those who do that are just irresponsible cowards. And that is why Krishna clarifies, "The renunciation of obligatory actions is not justifiable. The renunciation of them because of delusion is declared to be in the mode of darkness. He who, out of fear of bodily discomfort, renounces duty as it is painful, having performed renunciation in the mode of passion, surely does not obtain the reward of renunciation." [BG 18.7-18.8]

So what renunciation is in the mode of purity? The Lord says, "Whatever obligatory action is performed merely because it ought to be done, O Arjuna, renouncing attachment and hankering for the reward, that renunciation is considered to be in the mode of purity." [BG 18.9]

According to Krishna, this sort of conduct leads to liberation from all kinds of material enslavement. Those who act out of a desire for good outcomes will never be free of their karma. Depending on the types of actions they perform in their lives, the results — whether materially positive, negative, or mixed — continue to follow them even after death. To negate the consequences of their deeds, they must take one material birth after another. This is the perfect recipe to avoid liberation. Give up the desire for results and keep performing your duties. That way, you will always be free.

Before we wrap up for the day, I'd like to clear up a couple of misconceptions that many seekers have about the idea of renunciation.

A common question I get asked is, "Should I not expect my boss to pay me my salary? Should I keep working without expectation of a paycheck or profits?"

This is a typical layman's question. But I have the answer to this. To understand the concept of renunciation fully and properly, it is important to comprehend the meaning of *results*. Normally, the salary one gets or the profit one makes *seems like* the 'result' of his work. But is it really so? No, it's not. The result that Krishna talks about is the resulting change in one's emotional state. Salary results in happiness and satisfaction. Profits result in material joy. And we have already seen that, as a principle of self-realization, it is very important for one to be mentally stable in all circumstances. What Krishna means by 'results' is 'emotional results.' Of course, you should expect a salary every month in return for your services. If you do not get it, you should definitely fight for it. But that should be it. You should not be mentally disturbed by any means. That is the true meaning of renunciation.

Another question I often get asked is, "If renunciation does not imply giving up one's social or material life, why did Lord Buddha and Lord Chaitanya renounce their families?" This is a massive subject that needs an entire book for proper discussion. But for now, just understand that Lord Buddha and Lord Chaitanya had virtues way higher than the normal beings; and so the laws of material life do not apply to them. They abandoned their families in order to carry out even more important missions. We can't compare ourselves to them or expect ourselves to follow in their footsteps. We must abide by the rules that apply to us rather than those (if any) that apply to them. So instead of wasting time looking for a flaw in the Vedas that does not exist, we should concentrate on living our lives perfectly and fulfilling our mission.

Key Takeaways

1. Sannyasa (the renounced way of life) is 'giving up all activities done with the desire for results.' Tyaga (renunciation) is 'giving up the fruits of activities.'
2. Religious sacrifices, charity, and penance should always be performed.
3. You should never give up your prescribed duties, but perform them without expectations to derive any emotional benefits out of them.

Day 23: True Happiness

"One who is able, while still here (in this world),
before giving up the body, to withstand the impulses
created out of desire and anger, he is a Yogi; he is a
happy man." [BG 5.23]

Many self-help gurus advise their followers to be happy for no reason at all. They claim that happiness should not be based on external conditions, but rather on one's own internal state of mind. Though I agree that this is a better approach than relying on external circumstances to be happy, I disagree that happiness can be produced without a cause.

My approach is based on Krishna's suggestion in the Gita. Allow *Krishna* to be the root of your joy. To put it another way, let your *knowledge* of truth be the root of your joy. That is the most powerful method of ensuring eternal happiness.

There are several verses in the Bhagavad Gita where Krishna explicitly mentions what can make a person truly happy and what can keep a person from true happiness or bliss. Let's look at a few of them.

"That person attains peace into whom all desires enter, just like the waters enter the ocean, which remains ever undisturbed even while constantly getting filled; not the one who savors such desires. That person attains peace who, giving up all desires, moves about without longing, devoid of the ideas of 'I' (identifying himself with his mortal body) and 'mine' (material ownership)." [BG 2.70-2.71]

"I am the source of all; from Me everything evolves. Thus realizing, the wise engage in worshipping Me with loving devotion. With minds fixed on Me, with lives devoted to Me, enlightening one another by always conversing about Me, they (Krishna's devotees) derive contentment and bliss." [BG 10.8-10.9]

"When the mind, restrained through the practice of Yoga of meditation, attains quietude, and thus the self (ego) sees itself as the self (the soul), and finds contentment in the self (being an individual soul — a part of the Supreme Soul); when the Yogi experiences immeasurable bliss, which can be grasped by the intelligence and which transcends the senses, being thus established, he does not move from the reality (of being a soul). The state (of self-realization), once obtained, is considered by the Yogi as the gain beyond all other gains, established in which, he remains unshaken even in the mightiest sorrow. That stage is known as Yoga — the stage of freedom from pain. This Yoga should be practiced resolutely, with a steady and stout mind." [BG 6.20-6.23]

The Bhagavad Gita is not an ordinary book. It contains the perfect set of life advice meant for every human being on this planet. And if you want to know what it's like to be *really* happy, this is the book to read.

Krishna makes it extremely clear that for one to experience true happiness, one needs to be connected with the Supreme through meditation and devotion, giving up all material desires arising from ego. In other words, one who does not engage in Lord's devotion can never taste bliss. Meditation and devotion on Krishna are the perfect ways to achieve peace. In fact, these are the *only* ways to attain an everlasting state of peace and bliss. If you have come so far in this book, this should not be very difficult to understand. When you know Krishna is the source of *everything*, you obviously understand that Krishna is the source of happiness as well. If one is not connected to Krishna, then it is self-evident that one cannot experience true happiness.

One may seem content and peaceful, but without engaging in devotion, one's happiness can never be pure and lasting. But when one develops a love for Krishna, knowing fully well that He is the master and source of everything, serving the Lord becomes the source of the purest kind of happiness — the kind that is never-ending and limitless. Only those who have developed a genuine love for Lord Krishna, the all-attractive one, will understand this. Of course, this love should not be blind and baseless. It should be love in the knowledge of the loved. First, you should try to get to *know* Krishna (by reading the Bhagavad Gita). If you do this by keeping your mind open, welcoming, and free from prejudice, you will realize who Krishna is. With this knowledge, falling in love with Krishna will be effortless.

Once you fall in love with Krishna, your next step should be to try to *please* Him. There are a lot of things that make him happy — all simple yet, when done with devotion, very powerful. The simplest way to please Krishna and develop a love for Him is to chant His names. You should make it a habit to do this regularly. You may want to set a goal for yourself for how many times you want to recite His holy names in a day. Do this in the morning, for a few minutes during the day, and just before going to bed. This is the best way to satisfy Krishna, which will provide you with a great deal of fulfillment. It will help you control your desires for sense gratification, which is a must for gaining Krishna's association and love. I have given a few mantras while discussing the sixth principle of self-realization (Day 19), which you may want to use for this purpose.

Besides chanting the names of Krishna, you may want to read Srimad Bhagavatam to know more about Him and His various transcendental pastimes. Here you will learn about how and why the various universes (including the world we live in) were created by the Lord, and how and why He created various demigods, humans, and other forms of life. Here you will learn about His various incarnations as well. Reading with a pure heart will ensure that you fall in love with the various pastimes of the Lord. If you want to truly know the master of everything and everyone (I see no reason not to learn this except having a mind possessed by material longings), reading Srimad Bhagavatam is a must.

Engaging in just these two simple activities — chanting Krishna's names and reading Srimad Bhagavatam — will open your heart to Krishna, and thus Krishna will open His heart to you. Such pure love between a servant and the Master is the purest relationship in the entire creation.

I'd like to add one thing here. *Do not* make achieving happiness the aim of your life. If you chase happiness, it will always elude you, leaving you frustrated. Happiness should only come as a by-product of your actions in the right direction. Simply follow Krishna's advice in the Gita and you will experience happiness unlike any other.

Also, bear in mind that any happiness you will achieve in this material life will always be dwarfed by the happiness you will be able to experience once you have been liberated and have arrived at your true home. So your only prayer to Krishna should be to make you His associate and take you into His abode, where you can serve Him.

In verses 2.70-2.71 of the Bhagavad Gita, Krishna declares that a person who is engaged in the satisfaction of the senses can never achieve true happiness. I have already mentioned this while discussing the qualities necessary to achieve liberation. But here I would like to discuss this from a different viewpoint. Our senses are very limited, and so the joy and satisfaction which they can provide us are very limited as well. One can watch a movie and enjoy it. But can a person watch the same movie every day and derive the same amount of pleasure from it every time? Of course not. Can a person eat his favorite food every day, or in unlimited quantity? No. The movie and the food are the same, but the pleasure is reduced every time we consume it. Remember the law of diminishing marginal utility I mentioned?

But this is not how the love for Krishna is. Every time you hear or read about the pastimes of Krishna — the very same pastimes — your love for Him will increase. Every time you chant His name, you will desire to chant more. Every time you will start dancing in love for Him, you would not want to stop.

All you need to do is to *replace* your love for material things with that for Krishna. You will see the doors to endless love and happiness open up in front of you. Your desires will end there because you will realize what a waste of energy those desires are. You will be freed. You will be happy.

We have already seen that a prerequisite for attaining liberation is to offer the result of one's material activities to Krishna. This is not just a way to attain liberation from this world. This is also a way to stay happy while one is bound by the constraints of material life. The logic is simple. It is up to you to carry out your duties. But duties should never be done with the aim of obtaining the desired result. We should not forget that we are all Lord's servitors. So we should carry out our responsibilities, intending to dedicate them to the Lord. The Lord's joy is the only thing we should aspire for. Of course, this does not negate your duty to ensure the safety and well-being of your family and yourself. But you must remember you have no power over the results of your actions.

It's the outcomes that keep us up at night. Would I top my exam? Will I get a raise? Will my efforts be recognized? Will my father be impressed? Will I be able to grab that huge contract? Will the sale increase this month? You have done what you needed to do. Now sit back and relax. If you get a positive result, that's fantastic. If that doesn't work, try again. Never, however, be concerned, disappointed, or dissatisfied. If you're worried, disappointed, or moaning, it's a sign that you're still too attached to fleeting material belongings and accomplishments. And an overly materialistic person will never be truly happy. Be free of the results of your actions and devote all of your energies to Krishna. Then enjoy happiness for yourself.

Key Takeaways

1. Your happiness should be based on true knowledge of the self and Krishna.
2. Only a person totally free of desires for sense gratification and results of his actions can experience genuine and lasting happiness.
3. Recite Krishna's names and chant mantras having His names. Read Srimad Bhagavatam to develop ever-lasting love for the Lord.
4. Happiness, however, should never be the aim of your life but rather a by-product of the exchange of love between the devotee and the all-blissful Krishna.

Day 24: The Perfect Meditation

"A lamp in a windless spot does not flicker. This simile may be used to describe a Yogi, who has controlled his mind by the practice of meditation on the self (the soul)." [BG 6.19]

Today, meditation has developed into an enormous industry. We have thousands of meditation practices manufactured by so-called yogis (most of whom have no idea what yoga is) available on the internet. Meditation gurus charge exorbitant fees to teach the principles of meditation, claiming to relieve the meditator of all pains and miseries while also improving his concentration and memory.

There are a few things that need to be discussed and clarified here. So let's begin with a fundamental but very overlooked meaning of *yoga* (and *yogi*). What *really* is yoga? Yoga means 'to add.' To add what to what? To add the self to the Supreme. Yoga is a practice that is aimed at uniting oneself with the Supreme. And one who practices such actions regularly is a yogi. Easy, but most of us don't get it.

Yoga has been popularized as a combination of physical and mental exercise techniques to make and keep one's body and mind healthy and stress-free. This isn't yoga, I'm afraid. At best, this *can* be the beginning of yoga. It is easier to concentrate on the Lord when one's body and mind are in good shape. However, yoga should never be confused with simple physical activity to keep one's body or mind in good shape.

Now that you understand what yoga is, the next step is to figure out how to become a yogi, or someone who aspires to become one with the Supreme Lord. This we have already seen. Remember the four progressive steps toward Krishna — Jnana Yoga, Raja Yoga, Karma Yoga, and Bhakti Yoga? These are the prescribed steps to become a genuine yogi.

Raja Yoga, the yoga of meditation, is described in great detail by the Lord in Chapter 6 of the Bhagavad Gita. And a true seeker should understand the perfect method to meditate to make sure his journey toward the Lord is smooth.

Krishna, in the Bhagavad Gita, recommends that while meditating, a yogi should sit in a firm and clean place, that is neither too high nor too low, covered with grass and cloth. Thus seated, the yogi should focus on a single point, while keeping his senses controlled at all times, and be free from negative emotions, with the aim of self-purification. While meditating, his spine, neck, and head should be erect and firm, and his eyes should focus on the tip of his nose, and shall not waver. His mind should be free of any kind of contaminating desires like sex, and should focus on Krishna, fully considering Him to be his final goal. Whenever, during the practice of meditation, the mind of the yogi flickers, which it certainly will due to its inherent nature, he should bring it back to focus on the Lord.

This, according to Lord Krishna, is the perfect way to meditate for a true yogi, and one who meditates following this method will definitely succeed in attaining Him.

This is the perfect way to meditate if one is desirous of self-perfection and fulfillment of his real purpose. Of course, one also receives all the other material benefits of meditation while meditating in this manner. This type of meditation results in lasting peace, happiness, clarity of thought, and focus as side effects. But the primary goal of such meditation on the Supreme is transcending the material ocean and reaching the Godly abode.

Key Takeaways

1. Yoga is the process of joining oneself to the Supreme. A yogi is a person who seeks perfection through the attainment of the Lord.
2. Meditation on Krishna and His pastimes is the perfect meditation. Meditation is a spiritual

practice to become free of all earthly bonds and enter the true home of the soul, not a mental exercise to relieve oneself from tension.

Day 25: The Oldest Religion

"Arjuna said: By hearing that speech — the highest secret pertaining to the Supreme Self — uttered by You for my benefit, this delusion of mine has been dispelled." [BG 11.1]

Seekers often ask me, "Hari, you say that there is one Supreme Lord, and that is Krishna. Then why do so many religions exist in the world?"

To understand this, we would need to start from a time millions of years ago when the Lord gave the instructions contained in the Gita for the first time for the benefit of the entire humanity. In the Bhagavad Gita, the Blessed Lord says, "I taught this imperishable Yoga (the science of getting one with God) to Vivasvan (the sun-god); Vivasvan taught it to Manu (the father of humankind); and Manu passed it on to Ikshvaku (the founder of the solar dynasty in which the Lord appeared as Rama). This knowledge was thus handed down through orderly succession, and was received by the royal sages in that way. But, by long lapse of time here, the great science of Yoga was lost, O Parantapa (Arjuna). Verily, that same ancient science of Yoga is today told to you by Me, as you are My devotee as well as My friend. This knowledge is a supreme secret." [BG 4.1-4.3]

At the beginning of creation, Krishna spoke the wisdom contained in the Vedas, which is meant for all humankind. The word 'Veda' is derived from 'Vid,' 'to know.' Veda, therefore, means 'knowledge.' The Vedas reveal the essence of reality, including both the material and the spiritual realms, and carefully guide human beings toward the goal of God's love.

In *Bhagavad Gita - The Perfect Philosophy*, I have dedicated an entire chapter to prove how the knowledge contained in the Bhagavad Gita is truly the oldest philosophy ever, based on studies and research. So make sure you check that out.

Over time, Krishna's original message was lost. So Krishna, time and again, renewed His teachings, tailored to the nature of the residents of this world at particular times. He either came Himself, or sent His representatives, or empowered realized souls to speak on His behalf. We are all aware of the powerful messages of such incarnations and great souls.

We've already established that God is one, so all of God's laws are one as well. These laws are referred to as 'dharma' in Sanskrit, or 'religion' in English. However, this is not an accurate translation. Dharma can be described as the 'eternal nature' whereas religion means 'faith.' The nature of humans is all the same, irrespective of the time, place, and internal and external circumstances. This makes the concept of religion diametrically opposed to that of dharma. From the standpoint of dharma, the idea of God is not limited to one religion or one community of people.

Though God came in different forms at different times to speak in the way the people of those times can understand, He did not speak everything at all times. If you examine the philosophical ideas of all world religions and build a system around them, you will come across a hierarchy of collections of philosophical ideas that range from total to partial. And if you compare the completeness of all religions, you will find the wisdom given in the Vedas to be most complete. I can vouch for this as my claims would be backed by almost two decades of intense research on this subject. No two schools teach the same subject in the same manner and at the same level. Similarly, God's teachings at various times fit people's mental states and external situations at that time.

The thing that saddens me is not the presence of so many religions, but the role religion plays today. Religion today has become a tool to fulfill one's material desires. This has resulted in a flood of greedy religious gurus who profit from people's material motivations in the name of faith. While we need a certain amount of material fulfillment to be able to practice spirituality with peace, that should never be an end goal in itself. This is also a major reason for the spread of pseudo-faiths today. People are in dire need of mental support and are willing to pay large sums of money to anyone who can provide them with a brief respite, and these corrupt leaders gladly offer them the help they need.

In a nutshell, we have multiple faiths and religions because human beings use religion and God to fulfill their selfish material motivations. We cannot find the real dharma, which is intrinsic in all beings, eternal, and transcendent, unless we have a willingness to rise above this materialistic mindset.

The real dharma is *Sanatana Dharma* — the true religion of mankind. *Sanatana* means 'eternal' and *Dharma* means 'nature' or 'religion.' In verse 11.18, Arjuna, having realized Krishna's true nature, calls Him "the protector of Sanatana Dharma." This is our true religion, described in the Vedic scriptures. This is the religion that I practice and preach.

Now is the time to reconnect with your true self and take steps toward spiritual awakening. Don't get caught up in the whirlwind of distractions all around you. This is what Krishna wants of you.

Your time is very limited. Do not waste a second of it. The earlier you understand your divine nature, the smoother your spiritual path will be. There will be no ambiguity or uncertainty. And once the haze of your doubts has cleared, you will see a straightforward path leading to purity, devotion, and enlightenment.

Key Takeaways

1. Vedic wisdom is the true 'eternal religion' (*Sanatana Dharma)* that has always existed and will always exist.
2. The reason why so many religions exist in the world is that the Lord adapts His teachings according to the prevailing circumstances at various times and places.
3. Our task is to search for what is absolutely true and eternal, regardless of religious differences.

Day 26: Vedas or No Vedas

"To the Brahman (wise Yogi) established in knowledge, all the Vedas have so much use as has a small reservoir of water when there is flood all around." [BG 2.46]

I am about to tell you something today which may take you by surprise. I am about to tell you something which may look counterintuitive and controversial if you do not understand it well.

So pay attention.

KRISHNA DOES NOT WANT YOU TO STUDY THE VEDAS.

Surprised? I said you will be (I assume you *are* because that is the normal reaction I get).

I can already hear you shouting, "You write about and teach about Vedas and Vedic philosophy and Vedic sciences, and after so many days of religiously following your program, you tell me that Krishna does not want me to study the Vedas. Why is that? I don't understand."

You *will* understand.

The term *Veda* is derived from the Sanskrit word 'vid' which means 'to know.' So Veda means 'knowledge.' Thus, to gain knowledge, one should study the Vedas. That's all right. But the Vedas contain knowledge *of all kinds*, meant for distinct classes of men. In fact, Vedic literature is filled with knowledge about the different religious rituals that one may follow in order to amass an abundance of riches. It contains information about all that a person needs to do to fulfill any material desire he may have. The Vedas contain extensive texts on the topic of health. So, if you want to stay in shape and live a healthy lifestyle, you should refer to those portions of the Vedas. The Vedas contain information about all the demigods, including where they live and how to worship them in order to have one's wishes granted. The Vedas provide instructions about how to keep one's karma clean in order to have a better life the next time around. Essentially, it includes all the information that is deserving of the title of 'knowledge.'

But, according to Krishna, all of that knowledge is unnecessary if a seeker is seeking to understand Himself, God, their relationship, and the significance of his life. If one knows just this much, then no other information is needed. This much knowledge is sufficient to make one successful. It is because this knowledge is the ocean, compared to which the rest of the Vedic knowledge taken together seems to be just a small reservoir.

When you have access to the ocean, why would you need a well? The purpose of the well can well be served by the ocean. But no matter how big the well is, it can never serve the purpose of the ocean. Similarly, all other wisdom found in the Vedas pales in comparison to the knowledge of the soul and the Supersoul.

Most portions of the Vedas are aimed at fulfilling one's material desires. Krishna says that those who have a poor fund of knowledge utter flowery words out of over-attachment to the Vedas. Such intellectually challenged men are fixated on the material stimulation of their senses, believing that there is nothing more important to learn than how to fulfill material desires. They worship demigods to fulfill their own desires and also perform various religious sacrifices for material gains. True devotion for the Lord can never arise in the hearts of such ignorant men. That is why Krishna says to Arjuna, "O Parantapa, the sacrifice of knowledge (the practice of acquisition of divine knowledge) is superior to the mere sacrifice of material objects. All acts of sacrifice, in their entirety, culminate in knowledge, O Partha." [BG 4.33]

Krishna clearly states, "The Vedas mainly deal with the subject of the three modes of material nature. O Arjuna, rise above these three modes and the pairs of opposites (pain-pleasure, profit-loss, and so on), ever-established in pure spiritual existence, free from the ideas of acquisition and preservation, and be established in the self (the knowledge of being a soul)." [BG 2.45]

To simplify, learning the Vedas is a challenging and impractical method of approaching God. Krishna discourages it and favors the devotee who perfects his spiritual awareness while focusing his mind on devotion to God.

Vedic literature has been compiled by none other than the Lord Himself (as one can infer from verses 10.37 and 15.15 of the Bhagavad Gita). And so most seekers are perplexed as to why Krishna, the author of all Vedic teachings, advises against pursuing its principles.

Vedas contain *all* knowledge. And 'all' includes both 'material' and 'spiritual.' So not all information is intended to be absorbed by all. Those who desire material possessions can follow the Vedic injunctions that lead to material gains, and can thus derive material benefits out of them. And those seeking spiritual advancement (which is what the Bhagavad Gita is concerned with) just need to concentrate on the parts that have spiritual benefits. And that is what Krishna means to say in the Bhagavad Gita. Obviously, the Vedas should not be completely disregarded.

That would be a terrible mistake. Instead, the wise should choose and read portions of the Vedas that can assist them in breaking free from the endless cycle of birth and death and gaining God's association. If you find that difficult, simply reading and understanding the Bhagavad Gita and Srimad Bhagavatam will suffice.

The Lord favors the spiritual seeker desirous of only Krishna's association and nothing else. For others, there are a lot of benefits hidden in studying the *Karma Kanda* and other portions of the Vedas that can easily give a seeker of material profits whatever he desires. Vedas have everything for everyone. You can pick what you want, just like Arjuna picked Krishna, or Duryodhana picked Krishna's army. The knowledge is there for you. And the choice is always yours.

Key Takeaways

1. The Vedas contain all the wisdom that is worth gaining. Lord Krishna Himself compiled it through Ved Vyasa, His author-form.
2. The Vedas provide information on how to achieve material and spiritual prosperity. It is up to you to decide which parts of the Vedas to read.

3. The Lord favors one who chooses to gain knowledge of the self instead of knowledge about becoming materially prosperous.

Day 27: Putting Krishna First

"Whoever offers Me, with devotion, even a leaf, a flower, a fruit, water, I accept that, if it is offered by a pure soul with devotion." [BG 9.26]

As I have already mentioned several times, directly or indirectly, Krishna wants to see Himself as your first priority; because that is the single best indicator of the level of one's consciousness. A soul who is preoccupied with accumulating material possessions and treats God as merely a source of material comfort will not find a significant place in Krishna's heart. But one who puts Krishna first in whatever he does is the one who Krishna would love and would thus help to reach Him.

A devotee offers everything to Krishna first before consuming or using it. The material worth of what a pure-minded devotee offers is not important. What is important is the intention behind the offering. If one offers Krishna food before eating, it shows that he regards Krishna as his master, and always puts Him first. The food may be a very simple dish, but if offered to Krishna before eating, it becomes pure and nourishing. This type of food purifies the heart and brings one closer to Krishna.

Krishna acknowledges even the most insignificant offerings from a pure devotee, such as a leaf, flower, fruit, or even water. When water is given first to Krishna before being consumed, it becomes *amrut* (water that makes one immortal). A pure devotee thinks and acts in this manner. He offers everything first to Krishna.

The devotees of Krishna offer food to Him first and then eat it, considering it to be remnants of food eaten by the Lord. There is no greater joy for Him than to consume such purified food. Krishna is looking for this degree of devotion. At the very least, He expects the demigods to be fed first by seekers, if not Himself. That is why He says, "The gods, being satisfied by the performance of sacrifices, will indeed provide you with the objects you desire. But, he who enjoys what has been given by the gods without offering in return to them, is certainly a thief. Sages who eat the remnants of the sacrifices (food that is offered first as a sacrifice to gods) are freed from all sins; but the sinful ones who prepare food for their own sense-satisfaction incur sin." [BG 3.12-3.13]

The Lord considers the lives of such selfish sinners as waste. Such sinful souls, who just live for their own sake, and enjoy the gifts received from the higher authorities (demigods) without offering them in return, are unfit for advancement to the higher heavenly planets. Thus Krishna says, "One who does not follow here the wheel (of sacrifice) thus set rotating (by God), and who thus lives a sinful life, settled in the senses, lives in vain, O Partha (Arjuna)." [BG 3.16]

Krishna would certainly prefer a devotee, who after realizing the true nature of Krishna, being established in full knowledge and pure love, offers his all to Him. Such a devotee will be without sin and possess qualities beyond the grasp of anyone who lives selfishly for himself. Thus, the Lord advises Arjuna, "Whatever you do, whatever you eat, whatever you offer (in sacrifice), whatever you give (in charity), whatever austerities you undertake, O Kaunteya (Arjuna) — do that as an offering to Me. Thus, you will be liberated from the bondage of actions yielding auspicious and inauspicious results. With your mind steadfast by the Yoga of renunciation, being freed, you will come to Me." [BG 9.27-9.28]

This is what is needed — putting Krishna first in everything you do. Dedicate all of your deeds to Krishna to make them pure. This will cleanse both your heart and your past karma. You will eventually be freed from the bonds of material life and will be firmly settled in God's divine home, Vaikuntha, for all eternity.

Key Takeaways

1. Everything you do, no matter how trivial it may seem, do it as an offering to Krishna. All your actions will thus be purified and you will become a favorite of the Lord.
2. Instead, if you continue living for your own sake, consuming everything just to satisfy your material senses, you will only be doing yourself harm by drifting away from Krishna.

Day 28: The Unsuccessful Yogi

"Arjuna said: O Krishna, what happens to one who is
unsuccessful in Yoga — who had taken to Yoga with
faith, but was unable to control himself, as his mind
wandered away from Yoga?" [BG 6.37]

The Bhagavad Gita is the ultimate encyclopedia
for a true yogi. Without reading this divine work
of literature and fully comprehending the wisdom
contained therein, no one can achieve true
spiritual success in this material world. And that
is what this book (the one you are holding in your
hand) was aimed at — to make you understand
the success principles encoded in the Bhagavad
Gita and thus help you become a devout yogi.

But, having said that, it is not easy. No matter
how hard you try, success is not guaranteed. It is
not easy to make a complete mental shift. It is not
fair to expect someone who, until yesterday, was
preoccupied with pursuing material pleasures
and working ninety hours a week to accumulate
riches for the 'future,' to suddenly abandon all
material desires and devote his life to Krishna.
Even if one starts on the right track, life gets in
the way. It's not easy to keep one's mind free of
sensual impulses in the Kaliyuga. There are
distractions everywhere. And even Arjuna

realized that the path that Krishna wants us to tread is not going to be easy. That is why he inquired of Him about the fate of an unsuccessful yogi who, while beginning in the right direction, falters because of a poor materialistic mind.

A person who only hankers after material pleasures is the biggest loser. He can neither have peace of mind nor can enjoy the bliss of spiritual well-being. He finds himself in no-man's-land. Worldly pleasures are temporary, as we have already discussed several times in the past few days, and it is difficult to keep up with all the ways one can derive material joy. On the outside, he may seem to be enjoying and having fun, but on the inside he becomes weaker by the day, relying heavily on brief artifacts of transient gratification to achieve fulfillment. No amount of watching movies, playing video games, drinking, gambling, or having sex can truly satisfy a soul; because the soul is spiritual. It needs genuine spirituality to be truly satisfied. And we spend our entire lives chasing the wrong kinds of happiness. As a result, most of us end up in a precarious situation.

Consider a person who, after following the correct direction, becomes disoriented. It becomes much more difficult for him to derive gratification from material objects at this stage. He understands the difference between right and wrong deep down. He knows he has taken the wrong direction, leaving the correct path behind. Such a person cannot do either — enjoy material life and pursue spirituality; which seems to be a worse situation to be in.

But thankfully the situation isn't that bad. Lord Krishna has something in store for the unsuccessful yogi. He says to Arjuna, "The fallen Yogi, after entering the worlds of the virtuous (heavens), and living there for several years, is again born (on Earth) in the home of the righteous and the rich. Or, (depending on his previous spiritual progress) he is born in the family of the wise Yogis; verily, such a birth is hard to obtain in this world. There, he recovers the wisdom acquired in the previous body, and strives more than before for spiritual perfection, O beloved child of the Kurus. By virtue of the former practice (of Yoga), he is carried forward, in spite of himself (having no such inclination initially). Even one who merely wishes to know Yoga theoretically stands farther advanced than a follower of the ritualistic scriptural principles (described in the Vedas). And, by striving diligently, the reborn fallen Yogi, purified of sins, attaining perfection after the efforts of many lives, thereby attains the supreme goal (Krishna's association)." [BG 6.41-6.45]

Krishna tells Arjuna (and us) that a yogi who falters in the middle has a greater chance of reaching Him than one who never tries. In his next life, an unsuccessful yogi is born amid religious and affluent souls, providing a more fertile atmosphere for spiritual advancement. If he is fortunate, based on his previous efforts, he will have the rare opportunity to be born into the family of a perfected soul, making his mission simpler and increasing his chances of spiritual success. In this way, after many lives of progressing toward the ultimate goal, he achieves Krishna, the only worthy goal.

Phew! A long process, isn't it? But is it worth it? You bet. Is it necessary? No. But for that, you need to make sure you attain perfection in your current life. Why put yourself through so many births and deaths when you have the opportunity right now? And you have all the help you need. You have the Bhagavad Gita, you have Srimad Bhagavatam, you have so many wise souls to guide you, you have all the knowledge at your disposal, you have all the instruments to practice Bhakti, and you have Krishna. The only thing you don't have is a reason to avoid spiritual practices. Remember, there is no difference between one who cannot see and one who sees but does not act.

Key Takeaways

1. A yogi who strives for perfection but gets distracted gets a birth suitable for attaining liberation in the next life, and he keeps progressing in this way until he fulfills the purpose of human life.

2. It is highly recommended that, having been given this rare opportunity to attain liberation by being born as a human, one should try to do his best to break free from this cycle of birth and death in the current life itself.

Day 29: Enlightenment

"Indeed, this divine illusion of Mine, consisting of the modes of material nature, is difficult to cross over. Only those who take refuge in Me can cross over this illusion." [BG 7.14]

I'm so glad that I've had the privilege of guiding you through the highest and the most confidential of all knowledge for the past four weeks. This is the wisdom that we all have by default, but that we quickly forget when we come into contact with the world's material energy. Only a seeker who proves that he deserves this knowledge by sincerely enquiring about his true self receives the Lord's assistance in obtaining it. And I consider myself extremely blessed to have had the opportunity to serve mankind by spreading this enlightening knowledge through books and other means.

I define 'enlightenment' as follows:

Enlightenment (or consciousness, or liberation, or *Nirvana*, or self-realization, or self-awareness, whatever you may prefer) is that state of existence where the being is fully aware of the real identity of

the self, of everybody else, of everything else, of God, of the Universe, and is aware of how the Universe works and about the purpose of everybody's and everything's existence, and death.

The Bhagavad Gita contains all these insights. It has all the spiritual wisdom you'll ever need. It is, of course, a compilation of all Vedic wisdom found in hundreds of scriptures. However, reading such lengthy texts is simply not possible in our age. And the Bhagavad Gita is the ideal solution. It is only 701 verses long. It is easy to read through. You couldn't have asked for more from God. He has provided us with a fantastic shortcut to equipping ourselves with all the transcendental wisdom needed to cross this ocean of suffering called material life.

Understanding this single material full of the best life advice ever, coming from Lord Krishna Himself, is enough for one's spiritual upliftment. But if you want to learn more, you always have that option. Vedic literature is a never-ending reservoir of wisdom. Keep diving and you will keep discovering something new and amazing. But if you want a quicker method, then reading the Bhagavad Gita and practicing its teachings is the way to go.

And now you possess all that knowledge.

You are enlightened! Well ... almost.

Two things still remain for you to do before you can achieve perfection:
1. Surrendering to Krishna.
2. Practicing yogic principles as a way of living.

We will look at the first one today.

If you are one of those rare souls who have been able to grasp the truth contained in the Bhagavad Gita, then the next step for you is to surrender to the Lord (if you still haven't). This will ensure you do not ever deviate from the right path. Those who seek guidance from the Lord are guided. He never declines a pure devotee's plea for help. So you must first become a devotee and then surrender to the Lord.

Arjuna, having lost his composure, expecting evil results from the war, surrendered unto Krishna saying, "My mind is overpowered by weak pity and is confused about my duty. I implore You to tell me for certain which is the best path for me. Now I am Your disciple. Please instruct me, who has taken refuge in You." [BG 2.7]

When Krishna saw His disciple's complete surrender to Him, He gave him the best guidance ever by singing the Bhagavad Gita, His divine song. And you can imagine the result of listening to the Gita by reading what Arjuna said after hearing it from the Lord. Arjuna said, "O Achyuta (Krishna), my delusion is destroyed, and my memory (about one's true identity) has been regained by me through Your grace. I am firmly situated; my doubts are gone. I will now act according to Your word." [BG 18.73]

Can you see the difference? It's too difficult to miss. The Arjuna in Chapter 2 and the one in Chapter 18 almost seem like two different people talking. In the beginning, Arjuna was confused and anxious, shivering with tension, barely able to hold his famous bow, ready to give up everything, including his life, and with no hope. Then he turned to Krishna for help and took refuge in the Almighty.

This resulted in freedom from all doubt, knowledge of the true nature of the self and the Supreme, freedom from all anxieties, fears, and worries, and complete devotion to the Lord. What a transformation! Almost magical.

This is what real enlightenment is.

Key Takeaways

1. You must surrender to Krishna with a pure heart and ask for His guidance to attain the

most secret and liberating wisdom in the universe. You need to be Arjuna.

2. Simply surrendering to Krishna results in the ultimate enlightening knowledge and prevents one from getting deviated from the true spiritual path.

Day 30: A Vow to Practice

"Has this been heard by you, O Partha, with a single-pointed mind? Has your delusion, caused by ignorance, been destroyed, O Dhananjaya (Arjuna)?"
[BG 18.72]

You've made it right till the end, and I'm so pleased to see you on the last day of the program. From the bottom of my heart, I congratulate you on completing what you started. And I sincerely hope you gained a lot of benefit from reading those daily chapters.

Over the last twenty-nine days, you've learned a lot about your spiritual nature and relationship with the Supreme Being. This knowledge, believe me, is the most precious gift that you could have given yourself. This knowledge is gold. In fact, it is much more precious than gold.

THIS KNOWLEDGE IS EVERYTHING.

What could be more important than understanding who you are? Most people never get to know themselves, living their lives in denial and then passing away without ever contemplating the realities of life and death.

However, you are different. You are willing to find out the facts. And the fact that you've traveled so far shows that you're special.

So you have gathered the knowledge. Now what?

The next (and the final) step for you is to *practice* what you have learned.

Krishna explains, "Abandoning all desires, in full, born out of material purposes, and controlling all senses from all sides with the mind, he (the Yogi) should, slowly and gradually, become situated in tranquility, by his firm intelligence, his mind being established in the self, free from any other thoughts." [BG 6.24-6.25]

Enlightenment is not a result of a sudden spark in one's head, as is generally believed. It is the end result of a gradual process. If one does not follow the principles of yoga religiously, attaining self-realization is not possible. One needs to embrace yoga as a way of living rather than treat it as just a part of his life. And one needs to practice *all* the prescribed yogic principles like abstaining from material pleasures, engaging in Krishna's devotion, working without desire of favorable 'fruits,' maintaining a stable mind, being always established in the knowledge of the soul and the Supersoul, and so on.

Enlightenment will follow. However, one must put forward the effort solely to satisfy Krishna.

So, today, take a vow to practice what you have learned. Do not be a devotee just by name. Let your actions speak for your intentions.

And, to keep yourself on track, read a few verses from the Bhagavad Gita every day, because Krishna says, "And he who will study this sacred conversation of ours, I shall have been worshipped by him by the sacrifice of gaining knowledge; such is My opinion." [BG 18.70]

Study Vedic literature — the Bhagavad Gita and Srimad Bhagavatam in particular — and thus worship Krishna being established in the highest wisdom.

Never let your material life impede your spiritual life. Always remember that this is your opportunity, and your time is running out. So you need to get going *now*.

And if you immerse yourself in Krishna's devotion, all the bliss in the universe will surely be yours.

Key Takeaways

1. The Bhagavad Gita contains all the information that is needed for liberation.
2. To achieve absolute liberation from all bondage and everlasting association with Krishna, you must put all you've learned into practice and make yoga a way of life.

Conclusion

I am deeply thankful that you entrusted me with the monumental task of educating you about the Bhagavad Gita's vast knowledge. I had poured my heart and soul into writing and perfecting this book for it to become a single source of divine wisdom for all spiritual seekers worldwide. And it's incredible to see you stick to the program and complete it.

I sincerely hope you have enjoyed your journey through this book and that it has encouraged you to learn more about Vedic philosophy.

I hope, like Arjuna, you have become enlightened, at least partially, about the realities of your existence on this planet and your true nature. I hope you now understand God and your relationship with Him better. I hope you now have a clearer picture of the true goal of your life.

For me, it has been a pleasure to serve you. And for however much time I have left on Earth, I hope to be a dutiful servant of Krishna and all His devotees.

And for you, I have just one request in the end. Do not let life impede your spiritual journey.

Never! You have bigger things to achieve. And nothing could be a greater loss than not being able to do so when you still have the opportunity and all the necessary knowledge.

So, keep moving ... toward Krishna.

About the Author

Hari Chetan is a spiritual and consciousness coach and has an immense amount of experience in the fields of religion, spirituality, theology, and ancient and modern philosophy. He is an expert in all major religions and spiritual philosophies including Christianity, Hinduism, Islam, Buddhism, Sikhism, Jainism, Judaism, Stoicism, Zen, Taoism, and Baha'i. However, Vedic philosophy is his primary area of interest.

Having discovered the oldest and the most confidential spiritual wisdom contained in the Vedic scriptures, Hari is on a mission to spread this knowledge to all corners of the globe. His goal is to awaken the entire world to the true identity of the self and God, and make everyone aware of the purpose of their existence, as this is the only lasting solution to all our problems. He currently lives in Kolkata, India with his family.

Connect with Hari Chetan:

harichetan.com
hari@harichetan.com
facebook.com/HariChetanOfficial
patreon.com/HariChetan

A Gift for You

In the daily commotion that characterizes our lives nowadays, it is quite easy to lose track of oneself. And so it is important for us to maintain our mental equilibrium by connecting with our spiritual selves on a regular basis.

Download Hari Chetan's **free Bhagavad Gita Workbook** designed especially for the readers of his books.

This workbook will help you test your knowledge of the core concepts given in the Bhagavad Gita, and to keep you on track in your spiritual journey.

Try it. It's free to download and is very useful!

Visit **www.harichetan.com** to download.

The Bhagavad Gita Series

Book 1: Bhagavad Gita - The Perfect Philosophy: 15 Reasons That Make the Song of God the Most Scientific Ideology

Book 2: Bhagavad Gita (in English): The Authentic English Translation for Accurate and Unbiased Understanding

Book 3: 30 Days to Understanding the Bhagavad Gita: A Complete, Simple, and Step-by-Step Guide to the Million-Year-Old Confidential Knowledge

Book 4: The Bhagavad Gita Summarized and Simplified: A Comprehensive and Easy-to-Read Summary of the Divine Song of God

Book 5: Mind Management through the Bhagavad Gita: Master your Mindset in 21 Days and Discover Unlimited Happiness and Success

All Books: Bhagavad Gita (In English) – The Complete Collection: 5-Books-in-1

Printed in Great Britain
by Amazon